Collaborative
School Improvement

EIGHT PRACTICES FOR DISTRICT-SCHOOL PARTNERSHIPS
TO TRANSFORM TEACHING AND LEARNING

TRENT E. KAUFMAN

EMILY DOLCI GRIMM

ALLISON E. MILLER

HARVARD EDUCATION PRESS

CAMBRIDGE, MASSACHUSETTS

Library of Congress Control Number 2011941941
Paperback ISBN 978-1-61250-129-1
Library Edition ISBN   978-1-61250-131-4

Published by Harvard Education Press,
an imprint of the Harvard Education Publishing Group

Harvard Education Press
8 Story Street
Cambridge, MA 02138

Cover Design: Sarah Henderson

The typefaces used in this book are Minion Pro for text and Myriad Pro for display.

CONTENTS

FOREWORD

At a teaching team meeting a couple of years ago, Trent Kaufman said something that stopped me in my tracks. We were getting ready to launch the Data Wise Summer Institute at the Harvard Graduate School of Education—setting our team norms, reviewing our protocols, and building the team culture that would support us as we taught educators from around the world a clear process for using data to improve learning and teaching. We were feeling good about the program we had put together, and the mood had turned light as we realized that we had checked off the tasks we had set out to do before meeting that year's participants. And then, somewhat out of the blue, Trent spoke up.

"Can we talk about why this work is so hard?" he asked. "We all have a gut belief that zeroing in on evidence of student learning is the right thing to do for children. But if it is such a good idea, why is it so difficult to make it stick?"

While completing his doctorate at the Harvard Graduate School of Education, Trent had worked on the research and teaching teams at the Data Wise Project. When he graduated, he headed out into the world and began working with districts that were committed to bringing wise data practices to scale. Back on campus for what felt like a bit of a team reunion, he wanted to spend some of our precious time together addressing an issue that had clearly been weighing on him.

In the conversation that ensued, I saw the depth of commitment that Trent brought to this work, and the depth of experience that he was developing in the field. Whereas the Data Wise Project had been focused primarily on developing a process that would resonate with *school* leaders who were committed to using data to improve instruction, Trent and his colleagues set out to determine the role of *district* leaders in inspiring and supporting such a commitment in places where it might not already exist.

Several years later, reading *Collaborative School Improvement*, I see the fruits of his labor in taking on something that is really hard to do. This book contributes to our collective knowledge by offering a clear and field-tested set of practices for how schools and districts can structure their relationship to best serve student learning. I feel a kinship with the authors of this book because, as with *Data Wise*, they offer not a program to implement, but a paradigm shift in how educators approach their work. And, as we did with *Data Wise,* they offer a guide to making it happen.

As outside experts who have served a wide range of districts, the authors are in a unique position to make this contribution. In the space of just a few years, their roles have enabled them to work closely with districts that have different cultures and constraints but a shared determination to transcend them. This diversity of experience allows Trent and his colleagues to distill general principles with broad applicability.

But my guess is that readers will find that, even more than its principles, it is this book's concrete examples that they treasure most. In particular, I predict that chapter 9, which traces Chandler Unified School District's journey toward collaborative improvement, will be read again and again by anyone responsible for breathing life into this work. Within the text, exhibits, and figures of this chapter, the authors offer templates, calendars, guidelines, and even the strategic plan that the district submitted to its school board. This chapter represents a treasure trove of resources for launching and sustaining this work. Poring over these resources, district personnel will see how this work entails not just an audacious vision but also careful attention to detail in how the strategy is rolled out, who is involved, and when key decisions need to be made.

I also believe that the litmus test for Collaborative School Improvement offered in the conclusion will work its way into the broader public discourse around schooling. The authors here apply the term *litmus test* in a much more nuanced way than it is commonly used. Far from providing a simple "thumbs up" on implementation of the model, their litmus test offers a series of questions that will help district personnel engage in a deep reflection on its practice. Questions like "What do you know about the improvement work of the schools in your district?" and "How much time did you spend yesterday supporting your schools' improvement work?" do not invite the fudging of an answer.

This has not come as much of a surprise to me, and shouldn't to others who have worked with Trent and his colleagues. Asking tough questions is something they are not afraid to do. And, fortunately for us, neither are they afraid to work hard to find the answers. *Collaborative School Improvement,* in sharing their knowledge, will support the hard work that people in schools and districts are doing every day to improve teaching and learning for all children.

Kathryn Parker Boudett
Lecturer on Education
Director of the Data Wise Project
Harvard Graduate School of Education

Partnering for School Improvement

Alone we can do so little; together we can do so much.

—*Helen Keller*

Sir Arthur Conan Doyle introduced the world to a timeless partnership. *Together,* Sherlock Holmes and Dr. Watson were the perfect investigative team: Watson had people skills, the willingness to entertain Sherlock's games of deduction, and a genuine concern for the carefree Holmes; Sherlock had brilliance, persistence, and a flair for the dramatic. The unimaginative Watson would have never succeeded as a detective without Sherlock. Sherlock, with his hatred for the minutiae of daily life, would have likely stayed inside his Baker Street apartment, living in solitude, if it weren't for Dr. Watson! Their own words best describe how they valued each other.

In reference to Sherlock Holmes, Dr. Watson muses:

> [I]f I irritated by a certain methodical slowness in my mentality, that irritation served only to make his own flame-like intuitions and impressions flash up the more vividly and swiftly. Such was my humble role in our alliance.[1]

To Dr. Watson, Sherlock Holmes states:

> You are a conductor of light. Some people without possessing genius have a remarkable power of stimulating it. I confess, my dear fellow, that I am very much in your debt.[2]

A quick analysis of famous real-life pairs makes the compelling case that partnerships have the power to amplify individual capacity.

1

Political giants Jack and Bobby Kennedy combined guts, brains, and charisma to win a presidential election and then deliver arguably the most important positions of the early Cold War. Neither had all the ingredients alone, but their combination created a powerful recipe for success.

Bill Gates and Steve Ballmer pride themselves on a thirty-one-year business partnership that has kept Microsoft on top of a trillion-dollar industry that the pair practically created. As stories about them indicate, Gates and Ballmer complement each other—Gates is the big idea man, and Ballmer is the overachieving implementer. Together, they keep each other fiscally responsible and technologically innovative—a combination nearly impossible to find in the high-tech industry.

The realm of professional sports boasts many examples, but none more salient than Joe Montana and Jerry Rice of the 1990s San Francisco 49ers. Montana had the golden arm, but what good would it have done him without a receiver who could not only catch his passes, but also gain yardage afterward? Rice could shake off any defender anytime, but how many touchdowns would that have netted if his quarterback had not been able to deliver strikes?

In this vein, we believe the litmus test for an effective partnership is whether the parties together transcend what they could accomplish separately. We like to refer to this phenomenon as $1 + 1 = 3$. Outcomes were best when Jack consulted Bobby before a public address, when Ballmer implemented Gates's lofty visions, or when Montana placed a pass perfectly over Rice's shoulder after the latter had separated from his defender. These famous partners realized far greater success together than the individuals could have pulled off alone.

This book is about a similar partnership that has the potential for great achievement, but too often drops the ball: that between schools and districts. These two entities share a common goal in education: to improve teaching and learning in schools. Unfortunately, school personnel routinely wonder, "what has the district done for us lately?" while district leaders, in turn, wonder, "why haven't schools implemented the ideas we gave them recently?" This disconnect minimizes trust, paralyzes action, and inhibits each group from making the difference it signed up to make.

We know the school principal isn't Jerry Rice and the district leader isn't Joe Montana, but we have seen some amazing "educational touchdowns" take place—from double-digit gains in student proficiency in buildings where achievement had previously stagnated to districtwide student proficiency growth across all grades and content areas—when schools and districts pool their strengths. The practices described in this book will empower partnership between districts and schools, encouraging new collaboration toward districtwide improvements in teaching and learning.

THE NEED FOR DISTRICT-SCHOOL PARTNERSHIPS TO TRANSFORM TEACHING AND LEARNING

Recent rankings from the Program for International Student Assessment (PISA) placed U.S. students at a disappointing average in reading and science among industrialized countries, and below average in math.[3] These results—compounded by the persistent racial and economic achievement gap—highlight the need for reforming U.S. education *at scale* (across large districts or entire regions or states), which will require districts, not just individual schools, to become deeply involved in the work of transforming teaching and learning.[4]

The positive examples we have of improvements in student learning in the U.S., however, are usually isolated to individual schools that have broken cycles of poor performance by dramatically changing the way they've historically educated children. There are very few examples, if any, that demonstrate impressive gains in student learning at scale. Gradual improvements have been documented in a few large districts, but many of those can often be tied to major gains in just a few schools, changes in assessments, or, unfortunately, to evidence of gaming or even cheating the measurement system.

Is it even possible to generate measurable districtwide improvement on a large scale? This seems to be the crucial quandary in education, especially considering the absence of successful precedents. Our answer: "Yes! Definitely." This book provides the details behind our affirmative: it sets forth a proven method for quantifiable school improvement that can be adapted to each local district context. We recommend rebuilding the fundamental partnership between districts and schools, such that 1 + 1 = 3. In this light, schools and districts will see together the value each brings to the table. Like Watson and Holmes, each grouping of educational leaders embodies various strengths: districts have a big-picture perspective, while schools have deeper understanding of their local context. We have seen districts deliver stunning performances in the role of essential partner with schools: this is the vision we present for school improvement, and the practices required for that role are outlined in this book.

We are not the first to recognize the lack of productive relationships between schools and districts, nor are we the first to propose a partnership between a district and the schools it oversees. In a recent report written for the Wallace Foundation, Honig et al. document the need for districts and schools to come together for school improvement.[5] Their findings are clear: improving teaching and learning throughout a district requires the combined effort, talent, and other resources of schools and the district. The work of Richard DuFour and Robert Marzano highlights a similar point: the role of the district office is critical in building the collective capacity for transforming teaching and learning districtwide.[6] School improvement requires nothing short of an entirely new paradigm for the ways districts and schools leverage each other. Building on the work of these pioneers, our contribution outlines a concrete framework for what such a partnership could look like, and highlights many examples of that framework in action.

ENTER COLLABORATIVE SCHOOL IMPROVEMENT

Collaborative School Improvement (CSI) is built on the power of *inquiry cycles*.[7] Using inquiry cycles, schools can examine data to identify problems and develop relevant instructional solutions. Regularly collecting and analyzing data helps leaders build connections between teacher efforts and student performance. Although inquiry-based improvement has shown promise in developing a strong focus on instruction, variation in levels of implementation has yielded divergent results within and across districts.[8]

CSI is a set of practices, not a program. These practices enable districts to *collaborate* with schools to support inquiry-based improvements that extend across the district, rather than remain in pockets. Traditionally, districts have used formal professional development as the lever for supporting inquiry-based improvements.[9] While well intentioned, these efforts regularly fall short of making a direct impact on teaching and learning at scale throughout an entire district. One reason for this failure: professional developers often spend more time training individuals to access data, and less time providing strategies for using that data. These sessions rarely promote engaging with colleagues in the work of inquiry and instructional improvement. Therefore, professional development—at least as we know it—is unequipped to embed inquiry into school culture, or to cultivate a deep understanding of how data can directly inform instruction.

In this book, we propose eight concrete and replicable practices that enable districts to partner effectively with schools in inquiry-based improvement. These practices make up Collaborative School Improvement and address the cultural changes required for inquiry-based improvement efforts to deeply impact teaching and learning.

Our experience—first as teachers and principals, and now as outside consultants, trainers, and coaches supporting the districts engaged in this work—has given us a valuable window into effective implementation of inquiry-based improvement cycles. The aggregation of experiences in these districts illustrates both the challenges they encountered and the successes they experienced when they adopted new practices to support districtwide inquiry-based improvement. We witnessed firsthand that when schools and districts each gained a deeper understanding of how to leverage district support, they opened the door for substantial, long-lasting impact on student achievement across all schools. CSI provides clarity and direction in this endeavor.

Before introducing the concepts and format of our book, we believe it is important to clarify how we use three generally familiar terms in purposeful (and perhaps unique) ways. First, in our title we have chosen the word *collaborative* to describe a school improvement effort built upon a district-school partnership. Throughout the book, *collaboration* represents the strategic move toward this long-term partnership in the work of school improvement. The entire CSI model is saturated with purposeful collaboration—promoting productive teamwork among teachers, across schools, and between schools. Second, and also in the title, we identify our framework as a set of *practices*. Exceeding the scope of steps or processes, *practices* are ongoing and perpetually valuable. District leaders who have implemented CSI will affirm that it is not something they simply check off their lists; instead, it advocates a new way of doing business built on daily practices. Finally, we've called the teams that lead this work *transformation teams*. This descriptive name emphasizes the work that the teams do: they are the engine that propels the improvement process. Partnering with district transformation teams, school transformation teams lead the work that meaningfully transforms what happens in the classroom.

Each chapter in the book corresponds to one of the eight practices of CSI, and the ninth chapter documents a detailed, successful, three-year case study.

Chapter 1—"Adopt an Inquiry Cycle" To kick-start the process, a district (or school) must identify a data-driven inquiry cycle to guide its work. Because inquiry is the core of the process, this chapter articulates seven elements that are nonnegotiable in building a thriving inquiry cycle. It explains the importance of each element in relation to effective CSI.

Chapter 2—"Clarify Roles and Create Teams" Developing a working partnership between schools and the district begins with establishing clarity in their roles and corresponding responsibilities. Such clarity ensures smooth operation of a teaming structure—at both the district and school levels—which will in turn facilitate CSI implementation. In this chapter, we explore how the district selects schools to participate in CSI, provides ideas for the creation of its own team, and supports participating schools in creating their teams.

Chapter 3—"Team Effectively" Creating teams is only the beginning of building a district-school partnership that drives inquiry-based school improvement. This chapter offers techniques for cultivating collaboration within each team. It explores how the district transformation team can support school teams in learning to use time effectively, leverage the expertise of all participants, and develop coherence across individual schools in the district. With an emphasis on facilitative leadership, we explore how the practice of teaming effectively creates a structure for leadership within CSI.

Chapter 4—"Narrow the Focus" As an opposite of "boiling the ocean," the practice of *narrowing the focus* requires districts and schools to prioritize needs and allocate resources to best support improvements in teaching and learning within these areas. With a narrow focus, schools and the district are better equipped to understand and address root causes, making changes that will have a lasting impact on learning.

Chapter 5—"Lead with Purpose" Districts have a responsibility to lead schools through the challenge of improving teaching and student learning. In this chapter, we present seven key components of effective district leadership in the context of CSI: creating and maintaining a vision, modeling the work and how to effectively function as a team, teaching the required skills, providing relevant resources, setting high expectations, and providing regular and thoughtful feedback.

Chapter 6—"Connect Teams" The success of CSI depends largely on whether districts provide opportunities for participating schools to exchange ideas and innovations and to celebrate successes. Setting aside time for teams to come together and connect is an integral CSI practice. Connecting goes beyond allowing schools brief opportunities for sharing progress and discussing challenges; rather, it requires districts to identify best practices in participating schools and create meaningful venues for sharing those innovations for the benefit of all. This practice can be read as a subset of chapter 5, but its significance warrants separate and focused attention.

Chapter 7—"Leverage Expertise" Districts have long sought outside experts as they reach out to schools. In this chapter, we assist district leaders in reimagining these external roles, particularly with regard to the benefit and value outside experts can provide. We also discuss key characteristics districts should seek in external consultants, as well as strategies for helping those outsiders succeed. While outside experts can be very helpful, we emphasize that districts should plan for their departure from the beginning of the relationship, thereby keeping the focus on building school leaders' capacity and on gradually shifting responsibility from external to internal resources. Having acted as outside experts for several hundred schools and districts, we have a unique (and we believe, valuable) view into the material for this chapter.

Chapter 8—"Reflect and Refine" Districts sometimes focus too intently on implementing a new program with fidelity and too little on making the new program *their own*. Engaging in timely reflection generates opportunities for refining and developing the work of school improvement. Periodic reevaluation also shifts focus from the program to the desired outcome of the process—improving student learning. Using as context the experiences of three case study districts, this chapter highlights the program enhancements each district made as a result of its reflecting and refining efforts.

Chapter 9—"Implementing the Practices of CSI" Unlike chapters 1–8, chapter 9 does not detail a discrete practice. Instead, chapter 9 chronicles the journey of the Chandler Unified School District as it moved from initial excitement over a school-based improvement process to a fully baked CSI program for its entire district. Not intended as a blanket prescription for all districts, Chandler's experiences will nonetheless inform the work in your setting and provide invaluable examples and tools—especially as you take the first steps of your journey.

You'll also find a conclusion and afterword at the end of the book. Our hope is that the conclusion will provide an opportunity for us to virtually sit down with you and discuss your implementation of CSI. We ask a series of questions and consider some of your possible responses. The afterword is for those of you who want to know more about the research that supports CSI; in it, we attempt to chronicle some of the fundamental causes of ill-fated reforms and point to ways that CSI may help you avoid some of those common causes of student performance stagnation.

Chapter Structure

Each of the initial eight chapters is structured similarly. First, we present a problem common to many districts with whom we work. Then, we summarize the CSI practice that has successfully addressed that problem. The bulk of the chapter illuminates the practice by providing details, examples from the case study districts, and tips for implementation. Finally, the chapters provide a short list of takeaways that you can use as immediate learning tools during the first read-through, or as quick refreshers in future readings.

A Note on Reading This Book

Our recommendation is to first read this book in its entirety. As you read, you'll notice a distinction between the initial two practices and the remaining six. The first two should be implemented at the outset—and can be completed as if they were elements on a to-do list—while the remaining six overlap and, frankly, are never *done*. Then, as needed, you can review individual chapters, as each was written to stand alone. The practices of CSI are best understood in sum context; however, during implementation, you can review any chapter for tips about potential obstacles and useful ideas.

CASE STUDY DISTRICTS

Throughout this book, we reference three case-study school districts that engaged with us in the work of Collaborative School Improvement.[10] Each district has graciously allowed us to discuss its work publicly, for which we are immensely grateful. We had the privilege of partnering with these districts as they partnered with their schools; as outside experts, we enjoyed a unique view into each district's experience—one that we believe allowed us to be objective, thoughtful analysts within each district and across the set of three. These districts tackled obstacles similar to those you're likely to face in your setting, so we'll demonstrate how they addressed their problems by adopting the eight CSI practices.

The three case-study school districts are Chandler Unified School District (CUSD), Evansville Vanderburgh School Corporation (EVSC), and Portland Public

TABLE I.1

DISTRICT DEMOGRAPHICS

			Number of students						
School district	No. of schools	No. of students	Low income	White	African American	Asian/ Pacific Islander	Native American	Hispanic	Multiple/ Other
Chandler Unified School District (Arizona)	41	37,441	26%	57%	7%	9%	2%	25%	<1%
Evansville Vanderburgh School Corporation (Indiana)	40	22,498	53%	75%	14%	1%	<1%	3%	11%
Portland Public Schools (Oregon)	92	42,056	45%	56%	13%	9%	1%	16%	5%

Source: Gina Vukovich, Chandler Unified School District; Emily Smith-McCormick, Evansville Vanderburgh School Corporation; Data and Policy Analysis Department, Portland Public Schools, http://www.pps.k12.or.us/about-us/index.htm.

As of August 2011.

Schools (PPS). Following is a brief narrative description of each.[11] See also table I.1, which gives a quick snapshot of the student demographics of each.

Chandler Unified School District (CUSD)

A substantial suburb of Phoenix, Arizona, Chandler and the surrounding area is best known for the pleasant fall, winter, and spring climate. Chandler is also home to the corporate offices of some of the largest technology companies in the world. One challenge that Chandler has faced is its rapid population growth—about 10 percent per year since 2000—which has led to new schools opening nearly every year. Because of generally positive student performance results, some sense a general lack of urgency to improve the schooling of Chandler children.

In 2009, three CUSD middle school principals and a district director headed to Harvard for a weeklong summer institute through the Programs in Professional

Education at the Harvard Graduate School of Education.[12] During this experience, the team crafted a proposal to engage all district principals in a book study of *Data Wise: A Step-by-Step Guide to Using Assessment Results to Improve Teaching and Learning*.[13] In the year that followed, the team held monthly book study meetings and created a plan to involve a set of volunteer schools in CSI, using *Data Wise* as the vehicle of choice.[14] In their second year of work, the eleven original participating schools were thriving: each showed growth in proficiency of the focal subjects, and many showed double-digit growth in proficiency.

One element that distinguished the CUSD model was its regular cohort meetings (which were held monthly, as compared to every-other-month meetings in the other two case study districts). These meetings and regular "assignments" made it nearly impossible for the school transformation teams to lose momentum. Additionally, because schools volunteered for CSI—which required teachers to support their respective principal's application to participate—the CUSD schools had an extremely high level of ownership among teachers.

Evansville Vanderburgh School Corporation (EVSC)

The largest city in Southern Indiana, Evansville—often referred to as "River City" because it is situated along a substantial bend in the Ohio River—is home to one of the most progressive district leadership teams around. After participating in a cohort of the Urban Superintendents Program at Harvard University, Dr. Vincent Bertram brought his reform-minded approach to EVSC in 2007. Significant redesign of the central office's role has been underway ever since—particularly as Bertram began leading the entire set of forty Evansville schools through multiyear engagement in CSI.

At the conclusion of its first year, the district made adequate yearly progress (AYP) for the first time since its inception. After two years, the district results were astounding: every subject at every grade level showed growth! Significantly, fifteen additional schools made it into the most prestigious category of AYP, Exemplary Progress.

Evansville's model is an important case study for at least two reasons. First, EVSC chose to help all its schools through CSI simultaneously. This alleviated the pain that other districts felt from uneven CSI implementation. EVSC's choice allows us to discuss some of the tradeoffs in terms of breadth and depth of the work, along with the quality of individual support that the district can provide its schools. Second, this district's transformation team was perhaps the most complete of all the case study schools. As such, it sheds light on the difficulty of engaging in inquiry at the district level, as well as on the benefits of having a critical group of district personnel who fully understand CSI because they have done the work, as opposed to simply having planned, talked about, or read about it.

Portland Public Schools (PPS)

Portland, Oregon, is known for its environmental friendliness, coffee enthusiasm, and a school district that has led the way on several innovative educational reform fronts. In 2007, with generous support from Nike corporate leadership, the Nike School Innovation Fund dedicated financial resources and talent for five years to drive and support innovative practices in Portland, Beaverton, and Hillsboro public schools. PPS used its portion of the resources to cocreate, with Nike leaders, a five-year plan to engage its elementary and middle schools each year in school-based leadership development: the Portland Leadership Collaborative. This innovative program brought together administrative and teacher leaders to work effectively as a team to analyze student data and implement improved instructional practices to increase student achievement.

This collaboration led to a strategic thought partnership, enhanced teacher development, and increased student achievement. PPS's focus was to teach each year's cohort of schools to dig deeply into its student data and uncover core problems that could be addressed with a coherent action plan. After five years, all of Portland's K–8 schools would be exposed to a common school improvement framework, which would facilitate the work at scale across the entire district.

Portland district officials—in partnership with executive-level leaders from Nike, who provided resources in the form of human capital and financial investment—were intentional about several components of their CSI work that make PPS an important case study district. An independent outside evaluation, used as an initiative improvement tool, ensured that the work was focused on student outcomes, not just the engagement of educators. Portland used CSI to deliberately fit together various pieces of its strategic puzzle, including changing the school improvement plan to align with the inquiry cycle it chose, creating instructional resources in response to the needs of the participating schools, and integrating inquiry with other district initiatives, such as equity and response to intervention. By embedding Nike leaders on school-based teams, it was able to support the work by providing training in leadership development, strategic planning, out-of-the-box thinking, and focused messaging.

The work was part of the district's strategic plan, and therefore Portland carefully planned each cohort to build on the prior year's efforts such that all K–8 schools would have common experiences that would help the district achieve its lofty goals. Results of the efforts in Portland have been impressive, including double-digit gains in student achievement at many participating schools and significant, measurable gains in leadership skills and teacher collaboration.

SUMMARY THOUGHTS

Our work with schools and districts across the country has brought to light a large gap between what districts *can* offer schools and what they currently *do* offer. CSI creates a partnership, opening up the practice of schools and districts to enable each party to clarify and deliver on important roles. Without applying CSI practices or clearly defining the district's role in school improvement, district personnel may be left wondering how they can use their expertise in productive ways.

Our vision is that schools and districts will rely on each other's strengths for improving teaching and learning, much the way that Watson and Sherlock, Ballmer and Gates, Bobby and Jack Kennedy, and Montana and Rice partnered to accomplish great things. This productive partnership is clearly possible, as we've seen in the case study districts' experiences.

The work of early implementers—and the intuitive convergence of practice and research—has yielded dramatic and sustainable results, enabling us to codify CSI into the eight practices presented in this book. We are honored that you have chosen to take this journey with us, and trust that the time you spend exploring CSI—and your dedication to the practices contained herein—will yield dividends for the children and communities whose futures are influenced by your daily practices.

Together we can do so much.

CHAPTER 1

Adopt an Inquiry Cycle

Creating a Foundation for
Collaborative School Improvement (CSI)

Feeling great urgency to improve student outcomes, a new district leadership team in Evansville, Indiana, wants to enhance the district's relevance in school-level improvement efforts. To understand the historical relationship between schools and the district better, it gathered feedback from principals and teachers about the changes they would like to see in district leadership. One veteran teacher's voice rang loudly: "It seems that we have never had the time to try something long enough to gauge an accurate sense of its effectiveness. How could we know if what we were doing was having an impact if we didn't commit long enough to measure the effects? I am hesitant to try something new if I don't have a sense of how long it will last." This comment left the district team wanting to provide greater consistency in school improvement efforts and, in doing so, contribute more effectively to growth in student learning. The team's first question: where to start?

THE PROBLEM

It's easy to see how initiative overload backfires, actually decreasing the effectiveness of all improvement efforts. As the aforementioned teacher described, initiative fatigue dampens teachers' morale, rendering them less likely to align their instructional practices with the initiative of the season. Like a revolving door—always spinning in the new and out the old—a combination of changing initiatives, alongside a plethora of new programs that diffuse the attention of teachers and school leaders, results in minimal improvements. Responsible for presenting and support-ing each initiative, districts fret over medium to low levels of implementation. This becomes particularly troubling for districts because research demonstrates that even medium levels of implementation yield results in student learning that are no better than low levels of implementation.[1]

Without a firm commitment to a consistent practice from the district and across schools, the high levels of implementation required to deeply impact student learn-ing remain absent. During his first year as an assistant principal at a high school in California, Trent Kaufman (one of this book's authors) met with a veteran teacher and eagerly expressed his plans to implement new clinical observation practices to collect data on instruction. The teacher smiled slightly, checking his optimism: "Trent, I was here long before you came, and I'll be here long after you leave." Her response illustrates the long-term ineffectiveness of short-lived initiatives. Veteran teachers learn to simply "wait it out."

INQUIRY-BASED SCHOOL IMPROVEMENT

High levels of implementation correspond with consistent practice. Inquiry-based improvement cycles emphasize classroom-level changes that directly impact stu-dent learning. They equip teachers and school leaders to link data with instruc-tional decision making. By clarifying the process for teachers and school leaders to drive meaningful improvements in teaching and learning, inquiry cycles generate consistent practice that returns results.[2]

Inquiry cycles fuse data-based decision making and teacher collaboration in an iterative process designed to identify and target specific needs. By adopting an inquiry cycle that requires collecting and analyzing school- and classroom-level data, districts give schools the autonomy to identify and address school-specific needs. By zooming in—measuring and sifting detailed data—faculty members are able to identify crucial issues, prioritize real needs, and develop solutions that spe-cifically address those needs. Douglas Reeves describes this process as "weeding the garden."[3] Eliminating initiatives that fail to address high priorities (the *weeds*) boosts organizational effectiveness as the potentially successful initiatives (the *flow-ers*) receive necessary resources—particularly, faculty time and energy—to *grow*.

Educators urgently need access to tools that consistently produce long-term improvement in student learning, and research has affirmed the value of inquiry cycles in helping schools generate results.[4] When schools and districts engage together in inquiry-based improvement, they whittle away at the ineffective initiative pile and develop a shared process for strategically identifying, understanding, and addressing student learning needs. The districtwide inquiry cycle becomes *the* district initiative. In this sense, we're proposing a meta-initiative: Collaborative School Improvement proposes practices, not programs—a lasting mental shift emphasizing *that* districts and schools transform, rather than specifically prescribing *how*. What schools and districts do is determined by the inquiry cycle they choose to implement.

Like a structure built on a solid base, the practices of CSI are built firmly upon the foundation of inquiry-based school improvement. The remainder of this book explores how districts can effectively partner with schools to support the implementation of inquiry-based school improvement. The subsequent seven chapters will build upon this foundation, illustrating how each practice of CSI supports inquiry both within and across schools.

This first chapter guides a district in adopting an inquiry cycle that will determine the way that both districts and schools collect and examine data. We have briefly outlined three data-driven inquiry cycles that illustrate variations in steps and scale of interventions (see table 1.1). Collectively, they demonstrate that "implicit in all cycles of improvement is the connection between interpreting data and changing practice: the capacity to continually adjust or modify instruction based upon incoming data."[5] In CSI, then, teachers align their instructional practices with their data rather than with changing district initiatives.

ESSENTIAL ELEMENTS OF AN INQUIRY CYCLE

As outside experts and consultants, we have employed the Data Wise Improvement Process with great success.[6] All three of the case study districts employed this inquiry cycle. We simultaneously acknowledge that many inquiry cycles offer useful tools and structures for school improvement. Culling our varied professional experiences, we have identified seven fundamental elements of an effective data-driven inquiry cycle:

- Employing a step-by-step process
- Focusing on the *instructional core*[7]
- Targeting narrow, concrete problems and solutions that address a root cause
- Expanding the definition of data

- Using protocols and norms
- Making whole-staff decisions
- Monitoring progress

We recommend that districts adopt an inquiry cycle that includes these seven elements, or implement them in an inquiry cycle where they are not already present. Our experience shows that the exact inquiry cycle a district chooses matters less than the district's consistent emphasis on these key elements during implementation. Let's look closer at each element.

Employing a Step-by-Step Process

Teachers exist where the rubber meets the road in education, a reality that places seemingly endless demands on their time. From preparing lessons to contacting families to providing feedback to students, a teacher's day-to-day responsibilities require prioritization, which often means that nonimmediate needs remain unaddressed.

Using a step-by-step process provides a sense of the big-picture objectives while maximizing limited time. Transformation teams and whole school faculties both gain clarity and focus when they understand their progress in the context of the entire process. Keeping the end goal in mind, they can shift away from measuring only short-term increases in student performance and toward measuring meaningful, long-term gains in student learning.

Amid the urgency of school improvement, transformation team members in Evansville found that focusing on the individual steps—which, on their own, seemed feasible—helped to dispel anxiety about the larger inquiry process. While the overall prospect of implementing an inquiry cycle seemed daunting, teams understood how each step propelled them toward their goal. One participant noted several months into the work, "I used to think whole-school improvement work was overwhelming and just too much. The step-by-step process helps me realize that through each step, this work is manageable."

Additionally, an inquiry cycle that is broken down into clearly defined steps gives teams the advantage of knowing where they stand in the process, and knowing what work still lies ahead. This prevents stagnation: the cycle justifies and guides the next steps, situating them in the larger whole. Daniel Wertz Elementary School in Evansville used a visual of the whole Data Wise Improvement Process to frame faculty meetings, noting which steps the school had collectively completed and

TABLE 1.1			
INQUIRY CYCLES			
Inquiry cycle	*Commonalities*	*Distinguishing features*	*Number of steps*
Data Wise Improvement Process (Harvard Graduate School of Education)	■ Have iterative cycles that use data to identify school-based problems ■ Use instruction as the primary lever to address student learning needs ■ Emphasize planning for, and ongoing progress monitoring of, the effects of implemented changes ■ Use school-level data teams to implement the process, including examining data and identifying relevant instructional changes ■ Encourage collaboration, particularly among teachers	**Includes a "prepare" phase** that emphasizes effective teaming and assessment literacy **Observes instruction** as part of data collection to understand a root cause of student learning needs **Develops single, whole-school focus** instructional strategy to address a priority need	8
Decision Making for Results (D. Reeves)		**Focuses on both high and low achievers** with an emphasis on setting SMART goals **Identifies multiple strategies** to address prioritized needs	6
Plan-Do-Check-Act (P. Davenport)		**Employs tutorials** to target students at various levels of proficiency (geared toward reteaching concepts) **Facilitates enrichment** pullout to support students who have mastered content **Encourages instructional grouping** of students based upon their performance on standardized assessments	4

how the upcoming work fit into its larger goals. Displaying the eight steps of the Data Wise Improvement Process at the start of every meeting gave context to each step of the team's work. Looking at the big picture reduced isolation in each step and helped the faculty recognize progress—particularly as the school completed one full cycle and prepared to begin a second.

Situating their daily efforts within the big picture of a step-by-step process helps transformation teams clarify goals for meetings and set agendas that state specific objectives. These tools structure effective time use among transformation teams. In itself, this is a big deal: all educators can relate to watching minutes tick by in staff meetings where nothing concrete happens because the meeting objectives lack clarity and focus. With tools that structure time use effectively, the staff can see precisely how meeting objectives and tasks relate to the overall improvement work in which it is engaged. This is a dramatic, positive change.

A step-by-step process can support continuity from one year to the next. For instance, when faculty members reconvene each year, their tone is often one of "starting over" rather than building on the work from the prior year. In contrast, schools that ground their work in a step-by-step process use it to highlight the faculty members' work from the previous year and set the stage for new goals. By reminding teams of where they have been and where they are going, providing a road map that tracks progress from year to year, the inquiry cycle develops cohesiveness. When school transformation team members (STT) understand the step-by-step process and develop whole-faculty direction and purpose, they can drive meaningful changes in instruction.

Focusing on the Instructional Core

Most educators can point to a reform effort in their district that did little or nothing to improve student learning outcomes. Powerless reforms fail to comprehensively address the embedded nature of instruction, content, and students. This triangular relationship (see figure 1.1) has been documented by Cohen and Ball, and more recently by Elmore, in the exploration of the instructional core.[8] It is this core, which represents the very heart of interaction in the classroom, that provides the greatest lever for school improvement. Likewise, a failure to address the three components of the instructional core *together* misses the mark. Put another way, changing only one element of the core will not necessarily result in substantial improvements in learning. While these initiatives may be successful in making changes—like introducing new technology into the classroom—one cannot assess any measurable improvement in student learning related to those changes. For instance, a third-grade teacher uses a new computerized whiteboard to teach spelling but fails to utilize the technology to change the way she and students interact with the content. She uses the same lesson plans and instructional strategies, having only substituted the whiteboard for a chalkboard. Without changes to the instructional core, will there be any improvement in student learning for these third-graders? Sometimes

FIGURE 1.1

INSTRUCTIONAL CORE

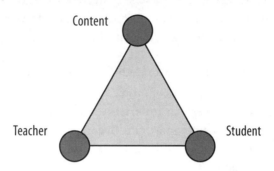

new curricula and technology do not advance student learning because they do not explicitly affect the way students and teachers engage with the content. Effective reforms, on the other hand, acknowledge that changing one of these pieces necessitates adjusting them all, and can therefore have significant effects on student learning.

Similarly, reform efforts that focus on training teachers will result in improvements for students only if those reforms improve teaching practice. Therefore, school transformation teams must explore the impact of instruction on deficits in student skills. Many data-driven inquiry cycles recognize this need and include specific steps for examining instruction. As teams explore the direct impact of teaching on student learning, they will begin to authentically address the instructional core. The most effective school improvement efforts actively leverage the instructional core to solve learning problems and deficits in instruction.

Schools across the country implement initiatives that address areas outside the instructional core. For example, school leaders who want to improve student learning might implement an action plan that includes providing study time for students during lunch, calling parents of failing students, and offering tutorials before school. Though they may have some positive impact, these strategies tackle school structures as opposed to instruction, and in doing so, fail to connect student performance with strategies that will influence the instructional core.

Alternatively, school improvement efforts are effective when leaders create meaningful action plans that strategically address both content and method—how teachers and students will engage with a topic and with each other. For example, teachers at Vogel Elementary School in Evansville identified teacher modeling as a strategy for improving students' writing skills. Vogel then created specific opportunities for teachers to collaborate to support students in editing and revising. Teachers developed strategies for modeling effective techniques with clarity and detail. Their plan utilized the inquiry cycle and maintained a laser-like focus on the instructional core, and it led to dramatic gains in student proficiency.

Targeting Narrow, Concrete Problems and Solutions That Address a Root Cause

Sometimes it's tempting to hack at big problems with a big stick—or, at least, with big reform measures. However, our experience shows that narrow solutions born of an inquiry cycle are frequently more effective for solving even large problems. If a narrow solution can specifically address a root cause, it will solve the larger problems stemming from that root cause.

In the 1990s, when Jerry Sternin and his team faced the overwhelming task of addressing malnutrition in Vietnam, they intentionally sought a narrow entry point to create their solution. While they acknowledged that poverty, lack of sanitation, and lack of access to clean drinking water were deeply embedded in the problem of malnutrition, they recognized that tackling these broad problems exceeded the scope of their resources. After making its initial observations, the team discovered that some families within the villages—though poor and living in the same conditions as their neighbors—were able to raise well-nourished children. Carefully examining these "bright spots," Sternin observed behavioral patterns that differed from those in the malnourished children's homes, and he identified a narrow solution based on those behavioral differences. Sternin's team noticed that families with well-nourished children fed their children four small meals a day rather than the two larger meals that were customary in most households. Additionally, parents with well-nourished children often hand-fed their children, ensuring adequate food intake. While changing eating patterns seemed like a small entry point for a large problem, the results of their team's solution were dramatic. Within six months, 65 percent of the children in the village were better nourished.[9]

The success of Sternin's intervention can be attributed to his finding a fine-grained solution that directly addressed a root cause. Examining the data, collected largely through observations, he and his team identified how feeding habits were directly influencing nutrition. Had Sternin simply supplied more rice—a solution that in itself lacked sustainability following his departure—without addressing this root cause (of active and frequent feedings), his story would likely have been lumped with the countless others documenting ineffective efforts to fight malnutri-tion. Instead, Sternin developed a foundation for powerful and sustainable changes in the communities in which he worked.

What do Sternin's experiences fighting malnutrition have to offer us in the domain of education? It is evident that Sternin faced major issues related to pov-erty, sanitation, and nutrition, but his successful solution didn't tackle each of those big issues. Instead, his solution was narrow and involved changing ineffective behaviors. His approach differed from common patterns in schools, where lead-ers implement multiple new initiatives in an attempt to address a broad range of problems. For example, a school might simultaneously implement a new math cur-riculum, transition to a new scheduling practice, provide new support to struggling students, and offer professional development on a host of literacy strategies. In try-ing to solve everything at once, nothing gets the attention it really needs, and ulti-mately nothing gets solved. Because the administration lacks adequate resources to support each initiative, educators find themselves exhausted at the end of the year, and with little to show for their efforts. Attempting to solve many big problems simultaneously is like trying to boil the ocean using individual stoves—lots of work involving lots of people but creating little overall change.

In schools and classrooms, educators—harboring a deep desire to improve learning for students but facing a stream of daily demands—are tempted to churn out quick solutions. Unfortunately, creating a solution—whether reteaching a con-cept, changing a schedule, or implementing a new curriculum—before adequately exploring the problem is like shooting in the dark. Simply put, without taking time for inquiry and collaboration, educators cannot identify a root cause or develop an effective solution: their well-meaning shots will fail to hit their target.

In practice, schools must prioritize data exploration regarding teaching and learning in order to narrow their focus and understand root causes. Narrowing the problem enables a team to intervene in a way that directly addresses the problem (see figure 1.2).

The identification of a narrow whole-school target—supported by shared under-standing of a root cause—concentrates everyone's efforts into an identified area of high need and drives collective action. When schools use an inquiry cycle to narrow their focus, they increase the potential for creating real improvements in instruction (for greater detail, see chapter 4). When a solution directly addresses a root cause within the framework of CSI, its impact becomes greater than its entry point.

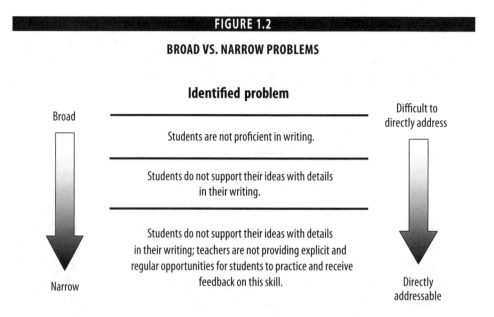

FIGURE 1.2

BROAD VS. NARROW PROBLEMS

Identified problem

Broad

Students are not proficient in writing.

Students do not support their ideas with details
in their writing.

Students do not support their ideas with details
in their writing; teachers are not providing explicit and
regular opportunities for students to practice and receive
feedback on this skill.

Narrow

Difficult to
directly address

Directly
addressable

Expanding the Definition of Data

Increasing emphasis on accountability in education over the past decade has brought greater attention to quantifiable data and pressured educators to help students perform well on standardized tests. While these data sources can offer some insight into student learning, they frequently fail to directly inform instruction. In fact, research shows that while teachers' access to data has increased in the past decade, measurable improvements in instruction have not. As noted by the U.S. Department of Education, "Even in districts with a reputation for leadership in using data, electronic data systems are barely influencing classroom-level decision making."[10] While electronic data systems provide teachers with massive quantities of data on student performance (much of which ends up posted in data rooms), rarely do numbers lead to deep improvements in teaching and learning. This disconnect can be frustrating for teachers and leaders alike, neither of whom have a concrete strategy for applying the information they receive from testing data. To develop a stronger relationship between data and practice, we suggest that districts and schools expand their historical definitions of *data*.

In fact, we suggest that the kind of data that really makes a difference in instruction comes from the classroom itself. While teachers frequently look at student work as a means to assess students, they could also use it to understand student thinking. In this light, student work provides teachers with the necessary context for making effective instructional decisions. Separate from assigning a grade, the process of looking at student work offers a lens into student comprehension, which is often a direct reflection on teaching.[11] When teachers can see how students are receiving instruction (as evident in student work), they gain a deeper understanding of the relationship between teaching and learning. In this way, teachers increase their capacity to use data to inform instruction. Imagine the possibilities for rubber-meets-the-road improvements when we harness this crucial, underutilized, classroom-level data. As data sources, student work and teaching practice more easily translate into informed pedagogical decisions than do the numbers presented in standardized student performance reviews.

We find that examining student work in relation to instruction frequently provides an *aha* moment for a faculty. Seeing a direct connection between teaching and student learning, faculty members find significance in sources they had not previously considered *data*. One participant noted, "So this is what data-driven instruction means! I had my doubts about how numbers could truly have an impact on my teaching, but now I get that data can be much bigger than that." By expanding the definition of data to include student work and instruction, we can better appreciate how they affect each other and influence the instructional core.

Classroom samples provide accessible, real-time data. Rather than waiting for quarterly benchmark data or annual testing results, which frequently arrive months after test administration, teachers can utilize classroom samples as needed to understand student thinking and adjust their instruction accordingly. Additionally, these sources are particularly accessible: it's easy for teachers to derive practical information from student work. One teacher reflected: "Digging into actual student work was useful, as we could get to know the 'real' student needs and thus better identify necessary and effective interventions."

Using Protocols and Norms

While financial resources—or the lack thereof—frequently receive attention in school improvement studies, our research shows that time is consistently the resource in highest demand. Many teams are involved in a myriad of efforts to improve learning, and they feel urgent pressure to make improvements. We acknowledge that engaging in data-driven inquiry requires time, but we've found that teams can minimize their overall time investment when they intentionally use protocols and established norms.

An inquiry cycle that utilizes protocols can mitigate demands on time by structuring both the *content* of meetings (how time is used) and the *procedure* (how to use that time more effectively). All educators have experienced that awkward feeling when people start shifting uncomfortably in their seats as a staff meeting goes twenty or thirty minutes over time. Simple tools—including agendas with clearly defined objectives and established time limits—can ensure that meetings are deliberately structured to generate solutions to highest-priority needs. Teams that *intentionally* use these tools in conversations and to distribute tasks can maximize effectiveness without increasing their overall time investment.

Protocols can "teach us habits that we wish we already had: to take the time to listen and notice, to take the time to think about what we want to say, to work without rushing, to speak less (or speak up more)."[12] While structuring conversations may feel counterintuitive to teams that are comfortable with their established patterns of dialogue, the effective use of protocols ensures that conversations support shared objectives. Rather than allowing dialogues about instruction and learning to become mired in the challenges of the profession, protocols direct conversations to that which is possible to control: the act of teaching.

Protocols also open up dialogue among faculty, ensuring a shared voice throughout. By outlining how time is used, protocols shift conversations from being driven by school and teacher leaders (or others who may naturally dominate) and invite all members to participate. This facilitates collaboration: it recognizes the value of each member and structures conversations to develop a team that, through full participation, is more effective than the sum of its parts.

Protocols direct teams to work on tasks where collaboration adds value. Much to the dismay of the math teachers with whom we work, we refer to this effective collaboration as $1 + 1 = 3$. In such an environment, teams use their shared time to accomplish tasks in which collective insight deepens the understanding and ability of the whole team. Unfortunately, without protocols, we find that many teams function as $1 + 1 = 1.5$, as tasks that can be completed individually are handled collectively. For example, one or two group members can easily create graphical data displays and then bring them to the team for review. Being deliberate about collective tasks can help teams use their time more effectively, saving them valuable hours.

Along with using protocols, we recommend setting and regularly revisiting group norms. When teams articulate which practices are most important to them, they support honest dialogue and build trust. Developing an environment where

---

BOX 1.1

TEAM NORMS

1. Be on time.
2. Participate; share your perspective.
3. Respect diverse ideas.
4. Stick to the agenda.
5. Delegate tasks evenly among team members.

---

everyone can interact openly is essential to promoting meaningful inquiry and reflection. Norms, like those shown in box 1.1, provide a guiding mission for the practices and values a transformation team should maintain in its collaborative efforts. Your norms will likely include more complexity than the example shown here, as they will reflect the unique makeup of your team.

We have found that as schools get the hang of using norms and protocols, they naturally begin to apply them to other elements of their work. As teachers, school leaders, and district teams leverage these tools to make purposeful use of time, they enhance a district's capacity to examine data and drive meaningful change for students.

Making Whole-Staff Decisions

Many faculty meetings become ineffective attempts at whole-school decision making. While it is important for leaders to value the input of the school community, teachers often sense that the principal had already made a decision but is trying to create the illusion of collaborative decision making, or, worse, that the principal lacks sufficient forethought to lead a constructive dialogue on the topic. Such meetings run long past their scheduled end and continue in dialogue for weeks or months without bringing true change.

Because whole-staff decision making is a fundamental piece of an effective data-driven inquiry cycle, doing it well requires new methods. Therefore, leaders must provide authentic opportunities for staff contribution and deliberately invite input in areas where it is meaningful. Let's look at how one school team made this happen.

When choosing a whole-school decision-making strategy, the transformation team at a school in Chandler effectively utilized faculty meeting time by completing

FIGURE 1.3

WHOLE-SCHOOL DECISION-MAKING

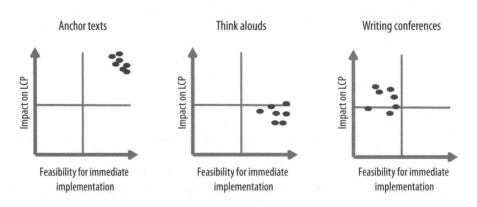

research prior to the meeting. The team members isolated three instructional strategies they believed would be relevant in addressing the identified student learning problems. Through a focused mini-lesson at the onset of the staff meeting, the team modeled each strategy. It then invited faculty members to add value by stating their opinions about the feasibility and impact of the various ideas on the table. To make a whole-school decision, the transformation team called on the staff's expertise (perception of the impact of the various strategies on student learning) and experience (perception of the feasibility of implementing each strategy). Their outcomes are shown in figure 1.3.

A well-planned meeting promotes staff ownership. With the opportunity to contribute meaningfully on a topic that directly affects their classrooms, teachers are more likely to feel invested in and committed to schoolwide changes. Whole-school decision making also facilitates changes that more accurately address the specific needs of the school. When all members contribute to the decision, the wider needs of the whole community—as opposed to those of a select committee—inform the outcome.

A strong school transformation team will facilitate schoolwide decision making by completing the background work for an open-input discussion. In the aforementioned Chandler example, the school transformation team took the initiative to outline three instructional strategies prior to the faculty meeting that addressed the problem of practice the school had identified. To provide a concrete framework for whole-school discussion, the team intentionally structured the schoolwide decision around feasibility and impact. The STT's preparation and planning paid off as it engaged its faculty in authentic and efficient whole-school decision making.

Monitoring Progress

According to the National Weight Loss Registry, those who experience the most success with weight loss weigh themselves daily. Clearly, the behavior in itself does not burn calories, nor does it force the person to choose low-calorie salad dressing. However, weighing oneself daily has important implications about the power of measurement. Research shows that frequent and consistent measurement keeps targets in focus, supporting ongoing adjustments as we work toward larger goals.

Measurement is equally powerful in schools: just as tracking weight daily encourages a dieter to stay committed, tracking school data helps teachers and leaders focus on their target goal. It is an essential element of an effective data-driven inquiry cycle. As schools get knee-deep in implementing changes to instruction, real-time measurements give them a clear sense of the effects of those changes on student learning. On the other hand, schools that wait for data from standardized assessments are left to perform an autopsy on their initiatives as they examine results that they cannot alter.

Monitoring progress eliminates the autopsy effect: it provides teachers and leaders with a sense of improvements in student learning throughout the work of Collaborative School Improvement. Most importantly, gathering timely and relevant data enables a school to make midcourse instructional adjustments based on what is or is not supporting improvements in student learning. With an expanded definition of data, as discussed earlier in this chapter, schools consistently have relevant and timely data sources available in student work. This classroom data enables teachers to develop an understanding of each student's learning, and thereby to adjust their instruction. *Data Wise* offers even greater detail, describing how to categorize student work into short-term, medium-term, and long-term data.[13]

Collected more systemically and at wider intervals, medium-term data provides the whole school with a shared understanding of the results of its work. A school in Chandler created whole-school awareness by generating a gigantic medium-term data chart that plotted a line for its yearlong goal and a line for its current progress as assessed several times throughout the year (see figure 1.4). Placed in a central location for teachers, students, and parents to view, the graphical data made the

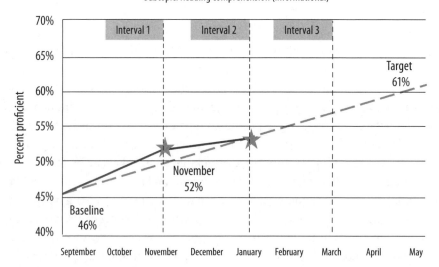

FIGURE 1.4

MEDIUM-TERM DATA CHART

Data source: NWEA MAP (Measures of Academic Progress)
Subtopic: Reading comprehension (informational)

information broadly accessible, promoting shared investment in and reflection on progress throughout the year.

Particularly in environments characterized by a strong sense of urgency, it's tempting to focus on dramatic short-term gains driven by efforts that do not create lasting and meaningful improvements to learning. We have seen this in several schools where students were instructed to restate writing prompts on standardized tests even if they wrote nothing else, as this assured them at least partial credit. While this tactic can certainly improve standardized test scores, it does little to increase student learning. Attempting to game the system is much like a dieter who strategically leans to the left side of the scale, knowing the imbalance will shave off a pound. While the number on the scale may be more appealing, the dieter has done nothing to improve his overall health. The practices of CSI and associated progress monitoring should focus on meaningful and lasting learning gains for students.

Assessing progress through the examination of short-, medium-, and long-term data builds a culture of awareness and responsiveness. This culture supports the habitual evaluation of the effects of programs—including professional development for teachers or student-based initiatives—in order to make appropriate adjustments in real time and effectively improve learning for students.

CONCLUSION

The adoption of an inquiry cycle as the foundation of their CSI work will provide districts and the schools they serve a concrete, step-by-step process for examining data, identifying needs, and addressing the root causes of those needs within the context of the instructional core. By effectively using protocols and norms to make whole-staff decisions, teams will expand the definition of data and monitor progress throughout the inquiry cycle. The specific cycle that a district adopts is less important than maintaining a diligent focus on the seven fundamental elements of an effective inquiry cycle defined in this chapter. Only through embodying these seven elements in practice will a district—and the schools within it—create a foundation for inquiry that results in deep improvements in teaching and learning.

■

TAKEAWAYS

- *It doesn't matter what color the coat is, as long as it keeps the wearer warm: the specific cycle a district adopts is less important than the implementation of the seven effective elements of a data-driven inquiry cycle.* These elements include using a step-by-step process, focusing on the instructional core, targeting narrow problems and solutions that address a root cause, expanding the definition of data, employing protocols and norms, making whole-staff decisions, and monitoring progress. These foundational elements will contribute to the efficacy of the work of inquiry-based school improvement. Leaders should maintain a strong focus on the implementation of these elements in whichever inquiry cycle they adopt.
- *A house is only as strong as its foundation: an effective system is prerequisite to systemwide improvement.* Data-driven inquiry cycles have the potential to create a systematic process for improving teaching and learning across schools. Inquiry cycles provide schools with effective tools for examining

data, identifying needs and their roots causes, and implementing relevant, targeted solutions. When faculty members expand the definition of data and gather it from various local sources, they are better equipped to make informed adjustments to their instruction. Using data in this manner gives teachers greater insight into student understanding so they can emphasize specific skills where students require additional support and use instructional strategies that target students' particular needs. Through analyzing data, teachers and school leaders will see what is working and what is not, and they can then more effectively allocate time, energy, and other resources to improve student learning.

- *Walk the talk: the implementation of a data-driven inquiry cycle is paramount to its adoption.* Adopting an inquiry cycle is only the first step in driving powerful school improvement efforts across a district. Thoughtful, committed individuals are crucial to driving the work forward and embodying the elements of effective inquiry cycles. In this role specifically, districts can be valuable partners in Collaborative School Improvement, providing the structure alongside relevant support for effective implementation.

CHAPTER 2

Clarify Roles and Create Teams
Organizing for CSI

In Evansville, district leaders return from a national conference with a new idea that they can't wait to share with their schools. They present the new initiative at a district-wide meeting at the beginning of the school year, assuming that with the significant momentum and good will from the session, as well as the leadership of school principals, school staff will implement the strategies with fidelity. Months later, when the district leaders visit schools to see how the implementation of the initiative is going, they realize that few of the schools are actually using any of the new ideas from the meeting. Teachers had every intention to implement the great ideas, but have lost focus among the many competing initiatives. School leaders did not view their role as "enforcing" implementation following the meeting. The schools didn't know they were expected to implement the initiatives because they were never explicitly told to do so, leaving Evansville district leaders feeling like opportunities to improve at the school level have gone unrealized. The district leaders wonder about their role—they have traditionally identified and offered resources to schools, but they hope to play a bigger role in school improvement without becoming a compliance group that mandates districtwide obedience to initiatives that may not be right in every local school context.

THE PROBLEM

Every educator we've met is invested in improving teaching and learning—that stands to reason. However, as evident in the preceding vignette, districts and schools are often unsure about which of them is responsible for various parts of the improvement process. Because school leaders are closer to classrooms, we've seen that they usually take charge of making school-level improvements. While districts have access to resources that could really support school leaders, district leaders are often not sufficiently connected with the improvements that schools are making to leverage those resources on the schools' behalf. Our experience shows that districts want to support teacher instruction and student learning, but they lack a defined role within school-level improvement efforts. Role ambiguity prevents the growth of an effective partnership between districts and schools. Defining roles means striking a working balance between autonomy and accountability: when districts provide schools with an inquiry process for data-driven decision making, they empower schools to identify and adopt relevant initiatives.

CLARIFYING ROLES

In many other processes, district and school roles are clear and complementary. For instance, district leaders typically partner with schools in hiring teachers. Districts often fulfill the responsibility of screening applicants, confirming credentials, and organizing interviews, while schools communicate personnel needs, interview candidates, and make final hiring recommendations. This partnership is effective because each party follows an outlined process that guides the hiring procedure: no one wonders who will perform which task or what will happen next. Everyone is accountable and follows the steps to accomplish that goal together.

Unlike the hiring process, school improvement efforts are nuanced and embedded in the specific context of a school environment. This chapter demonstrates how Collaborative School Improvement both *redefines* and *clarifies* the roles and responsibilities of schools and districts as partners in school improvement. CSI bridges the gap and demystifies the nuances: it offers schools and districts a clear structure for building a meaningful partnership dedicated to improving teaching and learning. The power of this partnership lies in *teams*. This chapter will explore the organizational structure of effective teams at both the district and school levels. Bringing the theory into practice, we'll highlight case study districts wherein leaders adopt an inquiry cycle and hold schools accountable for implementing it with fidelity. At the same time, we'll see how these districts leverage resources to support school autonomy in prioritizing individual building needs.

CSI roles become clear when all teams are functioning in sync: the district transformation team (DTT) supports the school transformation team (STT). In a nutshell, the work of the DTT is to embody all the practices described in this book—the details of its role will become clearer as you read on. Guided by the district lead, the DTT selects participating schools, which then build their own transformation teams. These STTs are responsible for implementing the inquiry cycle as described in chapter 1. Let's flesh out these roles a bit more and see how they drive meaningful improvement.

The Purpose and Role of the District Transformation Team

The DTT supports schools through the implementation of the inquiry cycle, providing resources in direct response to the focused priority needs that the schools identify. Rather than directing their energy toward mandating programs district-wide, DTTs support schools in focusing on inquiry-based improvement. Richard DuFour and Robert J. Marzano refer to this practice as *defined autonomy*, which calls for districts to define select and explicit expectations across schools while simultaneously providing school autonomy to meet those expectations.[1] In implementing the practices of CSI, the district defines the expectation of data-driven inquiry, while schools maintain the autonomy to address unique school-based needs they identify through inquiry.

While the district may have identified an inquiry cycle for implementation, it's hard to guide someone through something you've never done yourself. Therefore, the DTT engages in the inquiry process to learn firsthand where sticking points may arise. By running the cycle at its level, the DTT develops the ethos and wisdom to add value to schools' inquiry cycles. Additionally, having a bird's-eye view of many school processes at once equips the DTT to facilitate cross-school support as needed.

Emily Smith-McCormick, Director of Professional Development at Evansville Vanderburgh School Corporation, and her colleagues in Evansville witnessed firsthand the benefit of having a DTT intimately involved in supporting schools throughout CSI. She reflects, "You have a perception of how work should be done when you're on the periphery. It's not until you sit down and engage in the same work as the school teams that you understand how hard it is. When our district team engaged in the practices we expected of school teams, it qualified the struggles schools were encountering and helped us anticipate their needs as well."

Ongoing engagement in an inquiry process also informs the district's own work. For instance, as they partnered with school teams, district leaders in Chandler learned that the format of their assessment reports failed to provide teachers with instructionally relevant data. Through their inquiry process, the district leaders eliminated redundancies in their district assessment and created a tool that made relevant data available to teachers. Another example: in Evansville, inquiry informed the district's hiring practices. Through the DTT's interaction with school teams, it realized that its priorities in hiring principals with compelling personalities and strong, assertive leadership did not support whole-school, inquiry-based improvement efforts. In response, the DTT began instead hiring principals with strong facilitative leadership skills, which would be most useful to schools engaging in CSI.

When district transformation teams engage in inquiry, they are equipped to support school teams in this process. They also learn what elements are essential for effective team structure, and use this perspective to support schools in creating talented, diverse transformation teams of five to eight people. In addition to including the school principal or vice principal, balanced teams should represent a spectrum of grade levels and content areas. The DTT may help principals answer the following when forming teams:

- How many members will we have on the transformation team?
- What skill sets do we want to be sure we cover (data knowledge, technology savvy, etc.)?
- How can we best represent all grade levels and subject areas?
- Do we have any natural leaders on staff? Would they be willing to serve on this team?

At Bogle Junior High School in Chandler, principal Susie Avey used district recommendations to identify prospective team members with leadership potential (these recommendations are included in chapter 9 in box 9.2). She felt confident that they would represent diverse talents and perspectives well, building the capacity for the work schoolwide. Her final transformation team (see table 2.1) benefited from her DTT's experienced guidance.

Selecting a District Lead

The district lead is the person at the helm of the DTT, and the main liaison between the DTT, district leaders, and outside experts. The district lead ultimately serves as the eyes and ears of the district office, and will become the advocate for school needs as he or she begins to understand the big picture in a way that no one else in the district does. Box 2.1 highlights the attributes that we have observed in successful district leads.

TABLE 2.1

BOGLE JUNIOR HIGH SCHOOL TRANSFORMATION TEAM

Name	Role	Strengths/skills
Susie	Principal	Sets long-term vision; recognizes and taps into staff strengths and potential in order to build cohesive teams within and among staff; has ability to make/finalize decisions; is a data expert/manager; is an excellent communicator and motivator
Joe	Dean of Students	Possesses strong computer skills (for finalizing presentations); is able to create timelines and meet benchmarks for progress monitoring; conducts research specific to site goals and needs; is an excellent facilitator and is well organized
Jennifer	Assistant Principal	Is a natural facilitator, collaborator, presenter, and staff resource
Joy	7th/8th grade gifted language arts teacher	Possesses leadership skills; is a former department chair; is respected among staff members; has years of teaching experience; helped principal in initial two-year data push prior to Data Wise implementation; is a data manager
Phillip	7th grade social studies teacher	Is a department chair who is well liked by staff; is collaborative and promotes positive outcomes; is a strong presenter and creative thinker; has leadership skills
Regina	Special education resource/inclusion teacher	Possesses excellent organizational and computer skills (to aid in preparing presentation materials); is a critical and analytical thinker; is a data manager and talented presenter; is respected by peers
Khanh	7th grade science teacher	Possesses leadership skills; generates ideas; considers and elicits multiple perspectives; is a student-centric collaborator
Arlene	Math teacher	Is organized, analytical, and experienced

Source: Chandler Unified School District, Chandler, Arizona

In her role as district lead, Emily Smith-McCormick naturally engaged with individuals at all levels of the district in Evansville. She communicated regularly with the superintendent to inform him about the schools' inquiry-based work and to discuss his observations of qualitative and quantitative student data. She was open to input and ongoing feedback, and willing to adjust as needed to effectively lead her team. Because she had strong "soft skills," she was able to help the district

---

BOX 2.1

KEY QUESTIONS THAT DRIVE THE SELECTION OF A DISTRICT LEAD

- Does this individual have a clear connection with the superintendent and other individuals who are capable of authorizing changes within the district?
- Does this person have strong relationships within the district?
- Does this person have strong soft skills, such as problem solving and communication?
- Is this person open to learning and being coached? Is he or she receptive to ongoing feedback?

---

respond to school needs and acknowledge school successes. Leaders with soft skills—like communication, empathy, and capacity to motivate—support effective collaborative work. Table 2.2 lists some soft skills that are advantageous in a district team lead.

Selecting a District Transformation Team

It goes without saying that the district lead and executive leadership must thoughtfully consider how to structure the DTT, and which individuals are best suited to fulfill the roles. For some districts, organizing this team will simply require examining the existing structure of leadership. For example, where districts are divided

TABLE 2.2

SOFT SKILLS FOR EFFECTIVE LEADERSHIP

Communicating	Engaging in dialogue
Listening	Encouraging innovation
Solving problems	Making decisions
Delegating	Giving feedback
Motivating	Demonstrating empathy
Thinking positively	Showing self-awareness

TABLE 2.3		
DISTRICT STRUCTURES AND CSI		
District personnel organized by:	Geography	Department
CSI requires the district transformation team to:	Align roles	Rethink roles
CSI helps districts align with schools by:	Directly engaging with, supporting, and providing feedback to schools they currently oversee. If several individuals share schools, they may split these based on grade level (elementary, middle, and high), demographics, etc.	Pairing personnel with schools where they may have an existing relationship (for example, a Title I director engages with Title I schools), or have relevant experience and/or expertise (pairings based on elementary, middle, and secondary schools).

geographically, the regional superintendents could serve as members of the team. When districts lack an existing structure that could serve as a starting point for assembling a DTT, selecting individuals to serve on the DTT requires more thought and creativity to ensure that team members represent the whole district and align directly with schools participating in CSI. Table 2.3 provides direction about ensuring such alignment.

In addition to ensuring alignment with schools, DTTs benefit from including members with diverse skill sets. Our experience has shown that DTT members may not possess every desired quality. Therefore, it is imperative to carefully consider which attributes are most important. Based on our interactions with DTTs throughout the country, we have identified a number of nonnegotiable characteristics (as shown in box 2.2).

The DTT members provide support and feedback to schools while maintaining their functional responsibilities. With this in mind, districts will have to remove some of the DTT members' current loads so they can engage in and lead the work. Team members succeed when they can prioritize their work on the DTT; they struggle when their DTT roles become "just another thing" on their already full plates. Goethe's words are relevant to this issue: "Things which matter most must never be at the mercy of things which matter least."

BOX 2.2

SELECTING A DISTRICT TRANSFORMATION TEAM

District transformation teams containing members who meet these requirements are likely to build the capacity to lead CSI districtwide

- Facilitative leadership skills (as defined by Conley and Goldman, 1994)
- Some familiarity with the inquiry cycle their district has chosen to implement
- Experience with professional development
- Problem-solving skills
- Expertise in district data systems, as well as state and local assessments
- Instructional knowledge and classroom teaching experience
- Good communication skills

Selecting Schools to Participate

The DTT carefully selects which schools will engage in CSI, and when they will participate. Districts must decide whether to include all schools at once, or create smaller cohorts that involve different schools each year. In the multicohort approach, the DTT works with a number of small groups over a predetermined period of time; in the single-cohort approach, the DTT engages all schools within the district in CSI at the same time. To make this hefty decision, districts must consider whether they possess these essential resources: time to engage in the work, money to fund the work, and space to host teams during sessions.

The multicohort approach is more common and allows the district to allocate more resources to the seven to ten participating schools than it can if it involves all of its schools at one time. For example, finding meeting space was not a problem in Chandler because the district limited cohorts to a maximum of eleven teams in the first year of CSI implementation and eight teams in the second year. Using the multicohort approach alleviates other logistical issues that would be overwhelming in a single-cohort approach, such as aligning calendars, accounting for time away from the classroom (in the case of teachers serving on school transformation teams), and providing enough substitutes to cover classes. Selecting small cohorts of schools allows the district to reflect on outcomes and respond to needs on an annual basis, making adjustments that will enhance the next year's cohort experience. Following the first year of CSI implementation in Chandler, district leaders and outside experts refined their program by requiring that schools submit their work to the DTT for review, rather than to the outside experts as they had done in year one. This change made a big difference in building the DTT's capacity to lead the work and facilitated the partnership between schools and the district. By implementing small changes in the way that teams functioned and how the district held them accountable for their work, Chandler provided more relevant support to schools in year two.

Districts that use the multicohort approach can leverage the local expertise in cohort one CSI participants to guide school teams in later cohorts. In Portland, school transformation teams from cohorts two and three were frequently asked to attend cohort four sessions to share their successes, challenges, and insights. Such interaction builds the common cause throughout the district. The most prevalent challenge that district leaders face in a multicohort approach is being intentional when selecting which schools will participate in each cohort. Leaders must consider which schools are in greatest need of the support that CSI can provide, and which are most likely to implement the inquiry cycle with fidelity. Additionally, leaders must enact a strategic plan that anticipates and accounts for long-term variation in resource availability, employees, and executive leadership over the scheduled duration of multicohort improvement.

At the beginning of the 2008–2009 school year, district leaders in Evansville enlisted the help of an outside expert, and set out to train all forty schools in the district in the Data Wise Improvement Process, a set of steps for using data that includes both what we describe as an *inquiry cycle* and an initial phase that contains explicit guidelines for effective teaming and developing assessment literacy.[2] They chose to approach CSI as a whole district (single-cohort) for three reasons: 1) so that all schools could share a culture of inquiry in language and common purpose, 2) so that all schools could learn together the process and tools for using data to inform instruction, and 3) to respond to the existing urgency to improve outcomes for students.

District leaders in Evansville had to invest a great deal of resources—most prominently, time and money—to cover classes while transformation team members were in session, to allocate space for all participants to meet, and to align calendars. They also leveraged their DTT and outside experts in a herculean effort to train, provide feedback, and hold all forty schools accountable at once. While the single-cohort approach required additional planning and more midcourse changes to the district's CSI implementation than a multicohort approach might have, it provided a clear vision for district and school engagement. It also eliminated the hassles of selecting participating schools and planning for future shifts in district leadership and funding.

The Purpose and Role of School Transformation Teams

After the DTT decides which schools will participate, it helps each principal build a school transformation team. The STT implements the inquiry cycle by engaging the whole school in the process of identifying and exploring needs, detecting a root cause as defined by data, and solving narrow, concrete problems. As diverse members of the school community, the STT has the close knowledge and perspective necessary to guide the work at the school level. Supporting the school autonomy mentioned earlier in this chapter, the STT exists to lead the work within the school—engaging in the thoughtful planning required for whole-school decision making.

This teaming approach minimizes the inefficiencies of traditional whole-school decision making—where all faculty members discuss a topic, debate opinions, and come to a decision after a great investment of time—and the ineffectiveness of committee-based decision making. We've found that when committees make whole-school decisions, it is unlikely that the whole faculty will fully understand the committee's conclusions or their implications for practice. The STT *bridges the gap* and brings functional decision making to life. Unlike deciding on a new paint color for the auditorium or selecting a date for a whole-school assembly, decisions surrounding shifts in practice require sophisticated teaming. It is precisely this hybrid between traditional whole-school decision making and committee-based decision making that defines the role of the school transformation team. This teaming structure supports sustained attention by a majority of the faculty, a requirement of effective improvement efforts.[3]

By facilitating whole-school decision making, the STT repositions the relationship between schools and the district—from hierarchy to partnership. Traditionally, districts have targeted areas of need and prescribed relevant professional development. Within CSI, however, schools identify target needs and create interventions that address root causes. The district supports each school's work by aggregating similar school needs and providing resources (including time and professional development) in response to and in support of those needs.

THE CHALLENGE

Collaborative School Improvement rewrites roles and empowers real district-school partnership. CSI is a set of practices—not a program—that emphasizes school autonomy in identifying school-specific needs. Understanding this distinction is particularly important for teachers and school leaders who may be "mandate weary," having experienced a steady, changing stream of initiatives over the course of their careers.

CONCLUSION

Because CSI requires a departure from the traditional interaction between schools and the district, leaders must clearly articulate this, and collaborate with and support one another. Building transformation teams at the school and district levels will clarify roles and engender effective partnership. Dedicating their resources to either a multicohort or single-cohort CSI approach will enable district leaders (via DTTs) to offer specific, relevant support for school teams that will use data to identify problems, pinpoint their root causes, and lead whole-school decision making, thereby driving long-lasting, sustainable improvement.

■

TAKEAWAYS

- *Who's in charge here?: clarity regarding the roles of leaders and accountability for school improvement is essential to developing meaningful and effective partnerships between a district and its schools.* For substantive, sustainable change to occur, districts must hold schools accountable for implementing the inquiry cycle with fidelity, and simultaneously give schools the autonomy to identify high-priority needs and relevant solutions.
- *Choose wisely the leaders and the process: CSI facilitates intentionality in selecting DTT members and participating schools.* Strong leaders in district transformation teams empower partnership by providing relevant support to school teams to build the capacity for the work at the school level. After district leaders have clarified their roles and schools' roles, they will be

able to make an informed decision about whether to engage in a single- or multicohort approach to CSI.

- *The sum of its parts is greater than the whole: teaming within CSI creates a new process for schoolwide decision making.* Each school's transformation team facilitates whole-school decision making by implementing the inquiry cycle. The transformation team leads the work of inquiry-based improvement and engages the faculty in the process, driving whole-school ownership and coherence.

CHAPTER 3

Team Effectively

Building Skills to Engage in CSI

In the early stages of implementing their inquiry cycle, school transformation team members from a school in Chandler conduct twice-monthly planning meetings, but they have little to show for their efforts. At each meeting, members discuss pertinent topics critical to the implementation of data-driven inquiry. Everyone contributes valuable ideas, but their conversations carry over from one meeting to the next. Unstructured by agendas or clear protocols, the ongoing conversation inhibits the team's ability to make and act on significant decisions. As the months progress, team members feel frustrated, wondering why their time investment in inquiry fails to generate measurable improvements in student learning.

THE PROBLEM

Ineffective meetings breed ineffective teams, as members grow tired of a process that fails to maintain momentum and leverage time. As evident in the preceding story, when team meetings fail to accomplish objectives, the individuals involved lose value in the teaming experience. The main reason for working as a team is to accomplish more than the individual members could complete, an objective particularly relevant to the immense task of school improvement. Through all levels of a district, teams work to make a difference—from an executive leadership team to department and grade-level teams within each school.

Teams divvy up tasks among members at meetings. Ineffective teams rarely distinguish between tasks that are enhanced by collective effort and those that can be productively completed by an individual or pair. When teams assign tasks without intentionality, they fail to leverage the true power of collaboration. Ineffective teams also use meeting time poorly: for instance, some team meetings run long past their scheduled times or become mired in conversations on the challenges of the profession. Spending time on these topics can be cathartic, but it usually prevents the team from achieving its meeting objectives, thereby underleveraging the teaming experience.

Improving teaming is particularly difficult when the history of teamwork has not only been ineffective, but the decades of dysfunctional teamwork are so embedded in the school's culture that teams aren't conscious of the need to improve in this area. What's required is nothing less than a herculean effort, and we wrote this chapter to get you started.

Our experience shows that the district transformation team is the missing link: in itself, the DTT is a structure for meaningful collaboration, and it is equipped to support and lead school teams in fully realizing their collaborative potential.

TEAMING EFFECTIVELY

Productive teams make efficient use of team members' time and skills to produce results. Identifying and implementing an inquiry cycle creates the foundation for—but does not guarantee—the success of school improvement efforts. Success builds line upon line as the DTT reinforces effective collaboration at all levels of the district. The process of inquiry is only as effective as the teams that implement the work; it is for this reason that the *Data Wise* authors included a "prepare" phase at the beginning of the Data Wise Improvement Process, which builds a foundation for the effective collaborative work on which the inquiry cycle rests. Putting an ineffective team in charge of leading school improvement is like putting a typical fifteen-year-old behind the wheel of a Ferrari: the Ferrari's true potential comes to light only for a driver who has sufficient skill. The district is responsible for reinforcing effective skills in its teams, supporting their capacity to collaborate productively and attain results both in early stages of CSI and later as the challenge emerges of *sustaining* attention on collaborative work.

Unlike traditional school teams—whose interaction with the larger school community mainly involves reporting on decisions or transmitting information—transformation teams actually lead a schoolwide inquiry process. Their time together is directed by an overarching objective to engage the whole faculty in inquiry-based school improvement that leads to enhanced instruction. To simplify decision making, school transformation teams prepare data for whole-school analysis, identify protocols to guide conversations, and maintain focus on developing coherence and ownership schoolwide. The team can only fulfill these objectives when its structure embodies meaningful collaboration and effective use of time. District support is pivotal: it empowers STTs to accomplish their objectives through support for effective teaming.

You are likely a member of many teams, so you may be wondering how exactly the CSI concept of teaming improves upon your schools' existing structures of improvement. Here's the difference: we suggest that what often exists in schools are *committees*—groups of people who voluntarily come together for a shared purpose and whose time is largely spent discussing topics. In our experience, these groups focus primarily on the structures of schooling—schedules, attendance policies, etc.—rather than on the deeper context of teaching and learning. This may result in part from the difficulty of creating systemic changes with the involvement of only a small subgroup of the professional community. Simply put, without focused support on *how* teams should function effectively, school teams and committees engage in the same practices they always have, and will net the same *inaction* toward improvement in teaching and learning.

So, what we propose is a shift in focus: while identifying groups of individuals for specific tasks is not a revolutionary practice, CSI dramatically alters the responsibility and function of these school and district teams. CSI school transformation teams have a clear structure and are empowered to make a lasting imprint.

This chapter explores the essential components of effective teaming. More specifically, it discusses how the DTT can adopt these resources into its own practice and support teaming at the school level. The *creation* of teams, as described in chapter 2, is just the start of the process; high-functioning teams are necessary to sustain the inquiry cycle and general improvement efforts.

Facilitative Leadership Through Transformation Teams

In our experience, schools that achieve high-impact, widespread changes to instruction are those in which teachers drive the work of the school transformation team. CSI embodies facilitative leadership: it relies on the collaboration of diverse members of the school community, leaders, teachers, and other support staff. CSI cannot be implemented effectively by the principal alone.

Researchers David Conley and Paul Goldman define facilitative leadership as "the behaviors that enhance the collective ability of a school to adapt, solve problems, and improve performance."[1] The value of facilitative leadership exists in the *collective* nature of the endeavor. Without collective mobilization, teachers are less likely to feel ownership of the identified problem and instructional solution, and their implementation efforts will vary dramatically.

To expose STTs to the many advantages of facilitative leadership, the DTT must model this leadership style by using its authority to support professional give-and-take.[2] Perhaps new to some schools, the give-and-take nature of facilitative leadership lends itself to the existing structure of most districts where authority and autonomy exist in unison. Seeing the DTT engage in facilitative leadership will help each school community learn how it, too, can fit into the leadership landscape.

High-functioning teams require specific resources. Districts need to be aware that simply providing teams with the physical structure in which to complete the work—including an identified inquiry process and time to collaborate—will not suffice. Rather, districts can become powerful partners by supporting school teams in developing the tools to share leadership and collaborate effectively. Districts can also provide professional development that enhances team members' abilities to:

- Use time effectively
- Collaborate meaningfully
- Develop district and schoolwide coherence

These soft skills of inquiry-based school improvement complement the structure and process of an inquiry cycle, support effective implementation, and promote schoolwide improvements in teaching and learning. If the inquiry cycle is a seed, then using time effectively, collaborating meaningfully, and developing district and schoolwide coherence are the nutrient-rich soil.

Use Time Effectively

We've traveled to schools and districts across the United States and asked educators one question: "What is your greatest need?" The vast majority of them respond, unsurprisingly, "More time." As possibly the most valuable resource in schools, time is also usually in shortest supply. When teachers are asked to increase what they accomplish within their existing work day, the shortage of time can impede the effectiveness of school improvement efforts.

It's not a new idea, but it seems perpetually out of reach: how can we accomplish our objectives in a more time-efficient way? Our experience offers a few key strategies for leveraging time. First, teams can benefit from focusing on *what* they devote attention to (content) and *how* they devote that attention (process). Next, they can watch for unstructured minutes throughout the day and harness them to accomplish their objectives. For instance, we have observed that team meeting time frequently stalls in discussions on the day-to-day concerns of the profession; action gets buried in conversations about frustrating students, unresponsive parents, or the lack of time available to fulfill responsibilities (we can't help but point out that irony). As teachers and leaders adjust their behavior regarding unstructured time and focus on content and process, they will gain productive minutes to devote to high-priority needs. Two additional tools will maximize team productivity in the available time: creating agendas and implementing protocols.

Creating agendas

Using time effectively in team meetings begins with creating a focused agenda that defines objectives, meeting activities, and time allocation. The more details, the better: details tremendously increase the functionality of agendas, in part because they provide clarity during the meeting, but even more because they guide the planning process, structuring meetings around the highest-priority items. The district can support the effective use of time in school team meetings by modeling how to create and use robust agendas.

We frequently see the value of creating agendas when teams come together to make decisions collaboratively. When leaders craft an agenda prior to the meeting, they intentionally think about how they should allocate time to ensure that the team arrives at a decision by the end of the meeting. Group decisions are made more quickly when team leaders select a deliberate process for guiding input. How much time will be allotted to open discussion? What questions or topics will direct conversation? Will we try to reach consensus or vote? Our experience is that the time leaders invest in preparation for a meeting—particularly through providing a high level of detail—is easily returned in both the efficiency and effectiveness of the meeting.

You may already use agendas and wonder why we are reiterating such a simple point. Well, we've seen a few very effective teams leverage agendas as their primary tool to improve team functioning. These teams allocate time at the end of each meeting to collaboratively build the agenda for the next, which generates a shared ownership of the topics for discussion. Additionally, many effective teams create a "parking lot" where important but nonagendized topics are documented for a later time. The most effective teams create clear lists of action items that individuals are responsible for accomplishing and reporting on at the next meeting. Clarifying next steps and action items can push teams to identify specific tasks that individuals and/or the group must engage in to keep the work moving forward. This practice develops coherence about next steps in the work, promotes task completion, and distinguishes between those items that require the whole group's attention and those that can be completed individually or in smaller subgroups.

Agendas are only as valuable as their implementation. Effective agendas have the potential to improve how the team functions, but agendas that are not followed may actually hurt team functioning—they lack power and indicate mismanaged priorities. Simply put, to maximize efficiency in limited time, teams must vigilantly focus on the areas of highest priority, and well-executed agendas can lead teams to this pot of gold.

In Evansville, the DTT found that it repeatedly reached the end of its planned meeting times without accomplishing its objectives. Realizing that it was not driving its work forward but was instead becoming entrenched in the nuances of decision making, the team dusted off its secret weapon: agendas. The team created clear objectives, defined tasks for each meeting, and assigned an individual to create agendas and ensure their use during team meetings (see figure 3.1). The next time the DTT gathered and began to get off track in its discussion, the facilitator reminded team members of the meeting's objectives and the allotted time they had to meet each one. With clear time limits in place, team members felt increased urgency and more frequently came to decisions rather than carrying conversation over from one meeting to another. In the last five minutes of the meeting, the Evansville DTT set aside specific time to clarify next steps and action items that were assigned to various team members throughout the course of the meeting.

Transformation teams do not require the team structure to be utilized for all steps of the work. In fact, doing so can inhibit effective use of time. Unfortunately, we have observed that leaders frequently use as opportunities for collaboration tasks that can be accomplished more effectively individually or in smaller groups. For example, consider the inefficiency of using team time to make a data display. This task should not require six hours, but when it's completed during team time (with six team members over the course of a one-hour meeting), that's precisely what it consumes.

In contrast, we observed one district transformation team that applied team time where collaboration counted most. This team was planning to collect qualitative data on student learning through student interviews, and it needed to come up with relevant questions. Two team members volunteered to brainstorm interview

FIGURE 3.1

EVANSVILLE DTT AGENDA

Meeting: **District Transformation Team** Date/Time: **8/25/11; 1:00–2:00 PM** Location: OAA conference room	Facilitators: **Emily and Katie** Time Keeper: **Cathy** Note Taker: **Velinda** Action Item Keeper: **Frances**

Meeting Objectives:
- Discuss topics related to EVSC student dropout (ex. exit interviews, under 18 criteria, home schooling . . .) with facilitation by Marcia *Discuss high school programming that addresses the prevention of dropouts with facilitation by Tamara.*Review PM questions from last semester.

Agenda

Agenda Items	Time	Actor
DISCUSSION: Review previous meeting agenda and action items	5 min	Emily/Katie
DISCUSSION: Details related to student dropout collected by Student Services (special guest—Marcia) *Protocol:* Brainstorm questions/Presenter shares relevant information/ Team keeps notes of further questions to ask at the end of presentation **ACTION ITEMS**:	25 min	Marcia/ Emily
DISCUSSION: High school programs that aim to prevent dropouts *Protocol:* Same as second discussion item **ACTION ITEMS**:	15 min	Tamara/ Katie
DISCUSSION: Review PM questions *Protocol:* Members review questions and provide feedback related to current/ ongoing conversations using Plus/Minus/Interesting framework **ACTION ITEMS:**	10 min	Frances/ Emily
DISCUSSION: Determine roles for next meeting	5 min	Katie

Learner centered problem: Students need meaningful relationships with adults at school in order to be successful at school.

Problem of practice: The district does not have formal structures in place that promote and support meaningful relationships with students.

Source: Evansville Vanderburgh School Corporation, Evansville, Indiana

questions and present them to the team for feedback, employing the team's collective brainpower to enhance the list rather than to generate it. This process proved to be more efficient than brainstorming the questions as a group, and it illustrates strategic use of both team and individual time. In attempting to practice efficient use of group time, the DTT developed a keen understanding of how to coach STTs to be similarly thoughtful and efficient with their time.

Implementing protocols

Protocols also support the effective use of time.[3] Through defining procedures for collaborative conversations, teams have a clear path for staying on task and achieving meeting objectives. The value of protocols is particularly evident when district or school transformation teams collaboratively examine student work, or when these teams facilitate groups of colleagues to do the same. Because of their strong investment in student learning, teachers naturally focus conversations on student deficiencies and hypotheses for those deficiencies (many of which fall outside the realm of teacher control). The challenge is to drive these conversations to tackle the topic of instruction—which the teacher *can* control—and maintain a focus on action. When a meeting's content is left to the mercy of unstructured conversations or prior patterns of teamwork, the objectives are rarely met.

The district can be a valuable resource in providing schools with protocols designed to guide conversations and decision making, particularly in the context of inquiry-based school improvement. Giving schools these tools (and the know-how to use them) provides a method for meaningful collaboration, encourages the participation of all team members, and promotes examination of data that focuses on observation before analysis. However, like agendas, protocols are useful only to the extent that they inform practice. Because agendas and protocols can at first feel like an artificial presence in team meetings, providing opportunities for teams to practice using these tools can help them understand the tools' value. Structuring districtwide trainings around these resources can be an effective way to introduce and practice implementing these tools.

It is important to note that these resources challenge the existing patterns within schools. Directing the very structure of conversations—particularly through the use of protocols—requires shifts in practice. Teachers have explicitly asked why these new structures are necessary, particularly if those teachers have established collegial relationships with their colleagues over many years. We turn the question back to them, "What if using these structures could guarantee increased productivity and more effective use of time? Do you have any use for extra time?" Granted, imple menting these tools, as well as holding one another accountable for their use, takes time and deliberate attention. The investment returns dividends, however, as teams realize they are able to be vastly more productive in their collaborative work.

Collaborate Meaningfully

The structure of most schools in this country has created classrooms as silos, largely independent from one another.[4] Establishing classroom privacy as a culturally accepted norm has impeded many leaders' abilities to even envision how teachers can effectively collaborate with one another.

Over the past decade, however, researchers have increasingly identified collaborative culture as a necessary element of lasting and impactful school improvement.[5] The increase of professional learning communities (PLCs)—now mainstream language in the educational sphere—is just one piece of evidence illustrating this shift. The work of Newmann and Wehlage, which examined a five-year study of one thousand five hundred restructuring schools, linked qualities and practices of PLCs with reduced dropout and absenteeism rates, and with academic achievement gains in the core content areas.[6]

In a recent report, the National Staff Development Council identifies school-wide collaborative professional learning as a distinguishing feature between high and low performing schools that serve high-poverty populations. Through a review of existing research, the report highlights that "collective work in trusting environments provides a basis for inquiry and reflection into teachers' own practice, allowing teachers to take risks, solve problems, and attend to dilemmas in their practice."[7]

Within CSI, true team collaboration leverages the value of diverse team members. A group of team members who have diverse education, experiences, and skills can think through creative outcomes when the team faces challenges. Teaming is most effective when a variety of perspectives and ideas come together. Such genuine collaboration is particularly valuable within CSI because it supports the development of coherence (a topic addressed in more detail shortly) and provides the foundation for meaningful dialogue on instruction. While collaboration is undeniably valuable to school improvement work, and is a critical element of CSI, cultivating it requires specific attention. Structural changes (including common planning time) can facilitate collaboration, but they cannot guarantee conversations or efforts that drive teacher learning and improvements in instruction. Both structural and ideological elements may simultaneously impede valuable collaboration. As noted by research-ers Lawrence and Pauline Leonard: "Inherent in such a supposition [that teacher collaboration will be productive] is, of course, that teachers themselves actually retain commonly held beliefs about the value of collaborative activities and that they are able to avail of organizational circumstances and conditions that regularly generate them."[8]

Countless schools have implemented PLCs with little (or no) resulting change to instruction, which illustrates the necessity of intentionally monitoring and sup-porting collaborative endeavors. Without this support, individuals are likely to engage in the same conversations that have dominated common planning time in the past. The challenge lies in creating teams that engage in work *collectively*, not just simultaneously—teams whose voices are shared in the decision-making pro-cess, and whose conversations focus on improving teaching and learning.

Because teams already exist in schools (grade- and department-level teams, building leadership teams, etc.), leaders may assume that team members already have the skills for effective collaboration, so they don't bother teaching those skills within school improvement efforts. Besides, it can be complicated to show faculty members that there is room for developing meaningful collaboration, and that a shift in practices can enhance the team's ability to drive lasting and substantive improvements in their schools.

Districts can encourage team collaboration by offering professional develop-ment on effective team practices, emphasizing how they contribute to the inquiry cycle. At each districtwide training session on the inquiry cycle, teams in Evansville engaged in activities designed to promote collaboration. By setting aside this time for developing each team's collaboration capacity, the district openly values the skills that contribute to the inquiry process as much as the process itself. Providing teams opportunities to authentically engage in collaborative work—with the auton-omy to make decisions—reinforces the team as a meaningful entity, rather than simply as a symbol of collaboration. Districts can highlight valuable team skills and monitor progress by collecting data from teams about their functioning. Several districts with which we have worked have used an effective team practices survey (see figure 3.2) as a starting point for dialogue and reflection on team effectiveness.

We have also seen districts leverage a coaching model to foster collaboration within teams. Whether within the district or via an outside expert, coaches can provide an objective lens for observing team practices. Because of their distance from the immediate school community, they can support teams in staying true to the process. You can find an example of helpful feedback on team functioning in

FIGURE 3.2

EFFECTIVE TEAM PRACTICES SURVEY

This survey is intended to help your team discuss your progress as a team. When answering the following questions, consider the times when your *team meets to plan the work* (as opposed to the meetings that your team leads at your school). Circle the answer that most closely represents your response to the questions.

Does your **team**:					
1. Adhere to team-created group norms?	Never	Seldom	Sometimes	Frequently	Always
2. Start meetings on time?	Never	Seldom	Sometimes	Frequently	Always
3. Have a designated meeting facilitator?	Never	Seldom	Sometimes	Frequently	Always
4. Stick to the agenda and predetermined time limits?	Never	Seldom	Sometimes	Frequently	Always
5. Use time together for tasks that require collaboration (rather than tasks that could be completed effectively by individual team members?)	Never	Seldom	Sometimes	Frequently	Always
6. Keep the work moving forward (rather than allowing "sticking points" to inhibit the team's ability to progress?)	Never	Seldom	Sometimes	Frequently	Always
7. Set objectives and the agenda for the next team meeting?	Never	Seldom	Sometimes	Frequently	Always
8. Recognize strengths and limitations of the different personalities/work styles within your group?	Never	Seldom	Sometimes	Frequently	Always
9. Share the work load evenly?	Never	Seldom	Sometimes	Frequently	Always
10. Monitor and reflect on the effectiveness of your meetings?	Never	Seldom	Sometimes	Frequently	Always
11. End meetings with clear and specific resolutions and next steps?	Never	Seldom	Sometimes	Frequently	Always
12. Celebrate its accomplishments?	Never	Seldom	Sometimes	Frequently	Always

Do all **team members:**					
13. Come to meetings prepared?	Never	Seldom	Sometimes	Frequently	Always
14. Participate in team discussions?	Never	Seldom	Sometimes	Frequently	Always
15. Take ownership of the work?	Never	Seldom	Sometimes	Frequently	Always
16. Know what their peers are working on and how they can contribute to the collective good of the team?	Never	Seldom	Sometimes	Frequently	Always

an email that Trent Kaufman, one of the authors, wrote by request to the DTT in Evansville (see exhibit 3.1 at the end of this chapter).

Develop District- and Schoolwide Coherence

Ideas on instructional improvements are only as effective as their ability to penetrate classrooms throughout a school community. Therein lies a challenge—not only engaging in a process of inquiry to identify and address schoolwide student learning needs, but also driving a process that develops and sustains schoolwide coherence throughout the cycle. Coherence creates an environment where shared language and objectives exist, directly impacting courses of action and supporting improvements in student achievement.[9]

True collaboration, as addressed in the previous section, sets the foundation for developing faculty and staff coherence. When diverse team members engage with one another to lead the work of inquiry-based school improvement, it increases the likelihood that their work will diffuse into each department and grade level. Furthermore, the work of Collaborative School Improvement itself requires the team to engage the faculty in schoolwide decision making. The transformation team at each school frames the work, but relies on the participation and input of the whole faculty in making decisions throughout the process. Research on organizations emphasizes the increased productivity and quality of work that emerges when professionals work together on shared goals.[10] The school transformation team embraces this task.

Instructional coherence is a valuable outcome of the transformation team structure and schoolwide collaboration, yet it also deserves independent consideration from both district and school leaders. Cultivating instructional coherence begins with a high-level decision to streamline initiatives. As we have seen all too frequently, faculty members are often engaged in a myriad of initiatives, fragmenting their energy and focus. This fragmentation results in ineffective improvement efforts.[11]

To re-create the big picture from fragments, districts and school leaders benefit from having a common approach to school improvement that involves the entire faculty. This sets the stage for other behaviors that develop coherence. Schools that demonstrate high levels of coherence make investments—in both time and money—to further this cause.[12] These districts and schools focus their efforts on a small number of goals, rather than attempting to boil the ocean (a topic discussed in more detail in chapter 4). After identifying these goals, they are able to direct professional development and other instructional support toward those objectives.

Instructional coherence requires more than a statement of a shared vision for improvement; it requires opportunities for ongoing collaboration among the faculty. We've seen schools create this space in a variety of ways—from whole-school faculty meetings to grade- and department-level time to integrated PLCs. Designating time throughout the year for teachers to discuss data from student work or instructional practice is a necessary element to developing coherence. Such collaboration works best when teams have the skills to use this time effectively (as discussed earlier in this chapter).

Additionally, districts can emphasize instructional coherence within school improvement plans. For instance, through collaboration, the Portland DTT, Nike leaders, and the outside provider identified a need for focused messaging of school improvement plans. From this need, they created a template for schools to succinctly identify their school improvement focus, a tool that enabled schools to clearly communicate their school improvement plans, building coherence schoolwide (see figure 3.3).

Driven by the understanding that impactful changes in education occur at the classroom level, schools should designate time for teachers to learn and refine both new and shared strategies in the classroom. This should take place as part of, not independent from, the inquiry cycle—either to identify a root-cause problem or to monitor the implementation of the identified instructional solutions. Several of the districts with which we work have identified funds to support teacher release time so that teachers may observe one another's classrooms. These observations provide the context for conversations about implementation indicators, particularly as they relate to instructional practice. The district can further support this practice by introducing protocols for peer observation.

The very structure of the transformation team—a diverse team of faculty members at each school—emphasizes that a group of individuals must lead the inquiry-based improvement work in order for it to spread throughout the whole faculty. The district's role is to support the functioning of these school teams to enhance the implementation and effectiveness of inquiry-based school improvement.

THE CHALLENGE

CSI includes identifying a structure and developing skills that support the effective implementation of that structure. Transformation teams are central to the work of CSI because they lead their schools in implementing the inquiry cycle. When teams are functioning well, the inquiry cycle they lead will be more effective. Thus,

FIGURE 3.3

ONE-PAGER ACTION PLAN

LINCOLN ELEMENTARY SCHOOL

<table>
<tr>
<td rowspan="2">OBJECTIVE</td>
<td colspan="2">DEVELOP EFFECTIVE WRITERS
Help our students develop the ability to support their ideas with details in their writing</td>
</tr>
<tr>
<td colspan="2">GOAL: To increase schoolwide student proficiency in writing from 63% to 75% as measured by the 2012 state assessment</td>
</tr>
<tr>
<td rowspan="2">WHAT WE FOUND</td>
<td>LEARNER-CENTERED PROBLEM

Many students do not adequately support their positions with detail in their writing.</td>
<td>PROBLEM OF PRACTICE

Teachers do not expose students to complex and varied examples of exemplary writing throughout their instruction.</td>
</tr>
<tr>
<td colspan="2"></td>
</tr>
<tr>
<td>WHAT WE'LL DO...</td>
<td colspan="2">Teacher – Student – Content

Teachers will model the use of mentor texts to support their ideas with detail in their writing and will provide students with regular opportunities to use grade-appropriate mentor texts to support the development of students' writing</td>
</tr>
</table>

Source: Portland Public Schools, Portland, Oregon; Nike School Innovation Fund; Education Direction

the district should invest in providing direct support to teams as they learn to use time effectively, collaborate productively, and drive schoolwide coherence. These skills usually do not emerge spontaneously; rather, they require intentional focus and support.

Providing soft-skill support to teams can be challenging, however, because team members are generally unaware of what they lack. It's a case of "you don't know what you don't know." As a result, team members may question receiving support. We have found that modeling soft skills in district professional development and engaging teams in the work provides the most powerful opportunity for learning.

When teams discover the power of shared voice and the impact of true teamwork, they will embody these skills in their daily practice.

CONCLUSION

The work of CSI requires high-functioning district and school transformation teams. These teams lead the work at their respective levels and create a clear platform for communication between schools and the district. As a result, districts are able to offer relevant support and accountability to schools, and schools clearly understand their responsibilities and their lines of communication with the district. District and school teams use time effectively through implementing protocols, norms, and agendas. By collaborating meaningfully, they can develop districtwide coherence. The outcome of their investment is a productive partnership between schools and the district that better utilizes their collective resources to improve teaching and student learning.

■

TAKEAWAYS

- *One weak link makes the whole chain weak: inquiry-based improvement cycles are only as effective as the functioning of the teams who lead the work.* Providing a structure for inquiry is a necessary—but not solitary—foundation for driving meaningful improvements in teaching and learning across a district. School transformation teams breathe life into the process of inquiry. As a result, their ability to use time effectively, collaborate meaningfully, and develop district- and schoolwide coherence directly influences the extent to which improvements in practice take hold in a learning community. The development of these skills requires direct attention.
- *The only foolish question is the unasked one: the district can and should be a valuable resource in both monitoring and enabling teams to use time effectively, develop meaningful collaboration, and promote coherence in their schools.* The district and schools both benefit when resources are allotted to focus on the soft skills of school improvement. By placing importance

on cultivating these skills, the DTT conveys the message that teams (at all levels) must be willing to learn more than just the inquiry cycle in order to realize the vision of improvement efforts. Doing so requires skill sets that support a new way of doing business, and the DTT must lead by modeling soft skills.

- *Walk a mile in their shoes: creating and supporting effective teams requires an understanding of both the school transformation team's role and its work throughout the inquiry cycle.* Understanding the work of the school team provides a necessary lens through which the district can tailor its support. For effective teaming at the school level, the district must engage with schools regularly, develop an understanding of their work, and gauge areas where additional teaming support may be helpful.

- *No task is too small: effective teaming is relevant not only to school teams, but also to the DTT.* When the district prioritizes effective time use, collaboration, and coherence among its team members, it is better equipped to partner with schools in CSI. Simultaneously, through this process, the district comes to understand the very skills that benefit effective teaming.

EXHIBIT 3.1

FEEDBACK ON TEAM FUNCTIONING

Dear EVSC transformation team:

I enjoyed our visit to Evansville, and particularly enjoyed the time that we spent with the district transformation team. You all are asking the right questions and I get the sense that you will fulfill your important roles well.

You asked me to summarize the verbal feedback I gave today. I will try to do so below. Please feel free to give me push back, ask me questions, or engage in any type of dialogue around these concepts.

1. As we travel around the country, the #1 obstacle to the work of school and district improvement is time. It is with this knowledge that I give you the feedback on your transformation team meeting on Wednesday afternoon. You have a lot of years of experience and much talent sitting around the table, so it becomes extremely important to be productive with the time you have together.

2. I want to encourage you to clarify roles and responsibilities of the transformation team. These roles should be shared and should rotate throughout the year.

    a. *The facilitator's job* is to think hard about the agenda before the meeting. She should figure out which agenda items might require a specific protocol and how she will facilitate each agenda item. The facilitator should have a very clear vision of what the purpose of each agenda item is and therefore be able to deviate where necessary from the planned agenda when deviation is required to meet the purpose of the agenda items!

    b. *The notetaker's job* is to take very careful notes, particularly concentrating on the "action items"—the tasks that people commit to doing. The notetaker should send out the notes immediately with the action items clearly delineated. Each transformation team meeting should start with the notetaker reading the action items from the prior meeting so that the people who committed to discrete tasks have the opportunity to demonstrate or discuss how they accomplished their work.

    c. All other team members fulfill the following roles:

        i. Supporting the facilitator in accomplishing her role.

        ii. Offering to take on tasks and roles within discrete timeframes.

        iii. Providing feedback to the facilitator after the meeting with concrete and specific feedback elements. "Brenda did a great job" does not help Brenda get better. Rather, "Brenda, you did a great job! I really like how you tabled the discussion on graduation requirements because you felt that it would be best discussed once Dan was back from his conference. I also appreciated how you had really thought through the agenda item on clarifying the roles of the transformation team sufficiently that you were able to have those roles summarized on paper. That helped all of us provide suggestions for a final statement about our role and purpose." Specific feedback is one of the "culture changing" practices we are encouraging among school transformation teams.

3. One of the facilitator's roles (though anyone/everyone should speak up on this point) is to figure out what tasks are best done by individual team members and which require the attention of the entire transformation team. For instance, group brainstorms are typically most effective after someone on the team has thought hard enough about an issue or task to propose a specific direction. The group's job, then, is to take the individual's thinking to the next level—creating a "second idea draft" of sorts. If a group uses group time to think through issues for the first time, then all the group will ever produce is first drafts of ideas and deliverables. Facilitators should feel comfortable stopping the group and saying, "I think this discussion will be more productive if we ask Tamara to think through this issue first and bring back her best ideas for our input." Tamara's best thinking might stimulate the group to go in a completely different direction than they were headed. Tamara should feel pleased that the group has trusted her to apply her insight to this problem initially on their behalf.

4. Be sure to delineate between norms and protocols. Do you have team norms? If so, stick to them. If so, spend some time at one meeting per month checking in with each other and stating examples of times you have and have not behaved according to the norms. If you do not have norms, start creating and practicing them.

My sense is that these tasks will help you in at least three important ways. First and foremost, the quality of your thinking and work will improve, and your ability to help children in the district will grow. Second, you will be more efficient with the time you have, which will allow you to fulfill your other functions in the corporation. And third, your team will be able to master and model the very practices in which you hope school-based teams will engage.

I hope this helps. Please do not hesitate to reach out to me if you have any questions or want to discuss further.

All the best,

Trent Kaufman
Education Direction

CHAPTER 4

Narrow the Focus

Aligning Resources with Priority Needs

District leaders in Portland are excited about the newfound alignment among initiatives in the district. Different from prior eras, Portland is focusing its efforts on a few programs and communicating their connection at every opportunity. Nevertheless, following a leadership meeting in Portland—despite every effort to avoid this very concern—a district achievement coordinator rubs his brow, wondering how to support several initiatives. Drawing a deep breath, he confesses to his colleagues: "I'm concerned that with the districtwide focus on writing instruction, equity training sessions, peer collaboration, and the new math curriculum, the energy of teachers and school leaders is just stretched too thin." In his day-to-day interactions with teachers, he observes them actively working to implement the initiatives, rushing from one to the next. Yet, they can only do so much at once despite their deep commitment to improving student learning. "Teachers must feel as scattered as I do. I mean, I believe in the improvements the district wants to make with these initiatives, and I recognize the district's efforts to pare the list down, but I just don't understand how we can effectively do even four big things at once." As his colleagues nod in agreement, district leaders wonder why their efforts at alignment aren't trickling down as clearly to schools as they hoped.

THE PROBLEM

Carrying the immense responsibility of meeting the needs of a variety of learners, districts and schools regularly engage in a myriad of initiatives—from improving literacy, to making math instruction more relevant for students, to increasing culturally relevant teaching, to reducing dropout rates. Each initiative arises from good intentions, and each requires an allocation of resources to be effective. Not surprisingly, spreading even a wealth of resources across such a spectrum will diffuse results. And while a well-intentioned effort to make connections among initiatives is important, it neglects the root cause of the problem.

Without creating a focused, sustainable vision for school improvement, schools find themselves trying to boil the ocean—stretching their resources (time, energy, finances, etc.) thinly over many needs. As evident in the preceding story, multiple simultaneous efforts necessarily make for scattered implementation, even where leaders thoughtfully seek otherwise. Without a clear, data-driven process for assessing the most pertinent needs at each school, districts address problems broadly and superficially. In this situation, we fail to dig deeply into root causes or identify narrow entry points for addressing each need. It is no surprise, then, that in his research on more than two thousand schools, Douglas Reeves noted that "focus is a prerequisite for school improvement."[1] The inquiry cycle is the vehicle for identifying a focus. When we use it to uncover our most pressing needs and then deliver the bulk of our resources to address that need's root cause, we see results.

USING INQUIRY TO NARROW THE FOCUS

What we call for in Collaborative School Improvement is a fundamental shift in the way schools "do" improvement: instead of juggling many needs at the same time, CSI uses inquiry to determine which needs should receive attention first. In fact, CSI places inquiry at the center of all improvement efforts. Having a defined process for examining quantitative and qualitative data equips schools to identify and prioritize needs. Addressing only a select number of high-priority needs at one time enables teachers to focus specifically on those needs and make measurable gains in student learning.

In previous chapters, we discussed adopting an inquiry cycle and creating a teaming structure to lead the work at both the district level and within individual schools. In this chapter, we explore how the inquiry cycle can become the primary tool for identifying and understanding priority needs. It is through this lens that the inquiry cycle gains efficacy. As the foundation of improvement efforts within CSI, inquiry offers schools a clear process for narrowing their focus and prioritizing their needs. Rather than examining problems in isolation, inquiry-based improvement cycles start with the big picture and use data to narrow the focus—to identify specific areas of need relating to student learning. Refining the focus concentrates efforts in select areas, rather than dispersing a plethora of isolated initiatives.

When we start with a holistic examination of teaching and learning—beginning with high-level data and narrowing down to focal areas—we develop a deeper understanding of student learning needs. Recognizing a need to improve students' writing, one STT in Portland turned to inquiry to develop a more detailed understanding of the problem. Through engaging in the steps of its chosen inquiry cycle, this team learned that students who had low writing proficiency were most commonly unable to develop topic sentences. The identification of this root cause equipped teams to implement a targeted solution rather than tackling weaknesses in student writing generally via a new curriculum or lengthened instructional time. By focusing on helping struggling students construct strong topic sentences, the team was able to implement instructional strategies that made a significant difference in student writing proficiency.

Alignment

When we use inquiry as a starting point to identify needs, we have a context for prioritizing each identified need. Prioritizing allows us to explore root causes and allocate adequate, relevant resources to drive meaningful and sustainable improvements. It is precisely in this way that identifying priority needs not only provides for, but is also an essential element of, alignment.

Although discussing alignment of district initiatives is not revolutionary within reform circles, we propose a key refinement to that conversation: the practices embedded in CSI promote the *alignment of initiatives with school and district high-priority needs*, as identified through inquiry. This process of alignment concentrates energy, time, and other resources into areas of high need. Simultaneously, it requires schools and districts to abandon attempts to address myriad needs at once. The purpose—and the challenge—of narrowing the focus rings clearly in the words of Stephen Covey: "The main thing is to keep the main thing the main thing."[2]

Factors Influencing Initiative Overload

To understand the behavior that will drive a shift in the way we do improvement, we must first understand the behaviors that have informed current patterns in school improvement. We'll explore these within the context of the typical district. These patterns are based on our experiences working within and for districts across the country. It is likely that you have witnessed, experienced, and/or participated in some of these behavioral patterns.

In a typical district, a new initiative is frequently introduced because someone—either at the district or the school level—believes in its potential power for making improvements to teaching and learning. Maybe a school leader hears from a colleague in a neighboring district about the success of scheduling changes. Perhaps a district administrator visits a school implementing new math software and believes it would support student learning. Or maybe a department head attends a conference and becomes enthused about a new application-based science curriculum. These individuals have excellent intentions and usually have some evidence to support the efficacy of the changes they hope to implement in their department, school, or district.

These initiatives are designed to address an existing need. Chances are good that everyone in the school is aware of the need, but also that no one really understands the root cause of the need. This is a crucial point. Without taking the time to understand root causes, the likelihood of an initiative targeting true needs is diminished; implementing the proposed change is like taking a shot in the dark. This "ready, fire, aim" approach may have a positive impact in some areas, but will probably neglect areas of great need. For instance, adopting a new science curriculum will do little to improve science proficiency if the underlying problem is that students lack the fundamental math skills that apply to the scientific content. Providing professional development to support teachers in teaching the fundamentals of reading comprehension will do little to improve student performance if the root cause of the limited reading proficiency is fluency. If leaders fail to delve into the cause of student weaknesses, their proposed changes will have only a superficial impact.

Trent Kaufman witnessed firsthand a well-intentioned, shot-in-the-dark reform that drew from school resources but couldn't return on that investment because it lacked the data to hit the target. Departments at a high school where Trent taught were expected to request funds for resources directly related to the school initiative to improve adolescent literacy. At the meeting for departments' presentations to secure funding, the English department requested money to upgrade from VCRs to DVD players. The department representatives explained that the technological improvement would facilitate student understanding of novels. The English department received funding, but Trent questioned whether watching movies on DVD would address the deeper reasons that students at the high school struggled to master decoding and other comprehension fundamentals. He wondered how the English department might have sought resources to research the root causes of those issues and then address *them*, rather than simply upgrading its visual technology. When school communities lack (or misdirect) the resources to identify and deeply explore their needs, their solutions will fall short of addressing underlying root causes.

Digging a few deep holes can be hard to justify when entire acres need excavation. In other words, district administrators may neglect the search for root causes because their schools require improvement on such a broad scale. Typical districts may try to address numerous areas for improvement, in part, because the alternative presents a challenge. For example, when a district narrows its focus, it must justify its decisions to stakeholders, some of whom may view the narrowed focus as neglect of important issues. We hope this chapter helps you present solid rationale to concerned stakeholders.

Scattered, surface-level initiatives breed discouragement because of the dispersed focus and a lack of consistency across classrooms. Increases in student performance fall below expectations, and teachers and district leaders both become disheartened. When improvement efforts fail to yield gains, district leaders frequently abandon them in favor of the next initiative du jour. This response only exacerbates existing shortcomings: thinly spread resources, a lack of coherence, and a failure to deeply understand the root causes in areas of need.

CSI offers a new way of doing improvement that works again and again. It's sustainable, reliable, and rewarding. Rather than following in the footsteps of the typical district, CSI districts make concrete shifts in behavior to narrow the focus for improvement. Instead of requiring schools to tackle a diverse array of initiatives, district transformation teams support school teams in identifying priority needs and implementing focused initiatives that address root causes.

IDENTIFYING PRIORITY NEEDS

If we asked anyone in the school hallways or district offices what needed to be improved, we'd get a broad, perhaps bizarre, and often disheartening to-do list. Addressing each need on this list would require a myriad of diffused, Band-Aid improvement efforts. With so much to fix, focusing on one issue might feel negligent. Ironically, some of the same individuals who want more focus from the district chafe when it comes time to create that focus! At one training session, a principal in Chandler voiced her team's apprehension about narrowing the schoolwide focus

<table>
<tr><td colspan="2" align="center">TABLE 4.1</td></tr>
</table>

EXAMPLES OF PRIORITY NEEDS

Examples of high-priority needs	Focus for improvement
The achievement gap between male and female students in writing	Male students struggle to write a clear thesis and to support the thesis with details.
Poor reading comprehension skills in grades 6–8	Students struggle to draw inferences from fictional text.
Weaknesses in number sense in the elementary grades	Students struggle to understand and apply the concept of place value.

to a particular area of student learning, which teachers had identified by looking at both quantitative and qualitative student performance data:

> We know that many of our students are struggling with understanding vocabulary and summarizing expository texts—it was clear when we looked at our state test data and student work that this was an area in which we needed to focus. What we're struggling with the most is the idea that, if we focus our efforts on this one area, we're neglecting other student learning needs. How can we "ignore" other subject areas and feel like we're fulfilling our responsibilities as educators?

While the temptation to simultaneously address multiple needs is understandable— particularly when student outcomes are involved—this approach consistently yields disappointing results. CSI certainly doesn't advocate focusing on one element of education and neglecting the rest; rather, CSI ties improvement efforts directly to *priority needs*. Priority needs are areas in which improvement will most benefit students—either because of a particularly deep disparity in student learning, or because there is widespread need across a high number of students (see table 4.1).

Determining priority needs is obviously complex and, as illustrated by the Chandler principal, schools are likely to struggle with teasing them out. It is unlikely that one or two priority needs will distinguish themselves from others. CSI is not a process of finding the "right" needs, but rather of using data—per the inquiry cycle you choose—to intentionally identify focused and narrow needs that have the potential to bring about widespread improvements for students. Leaders can then commit to focusing on those needs with the majority of resources, thus increasing the capacity for real improvement.

ALIGNING INITIATIVES WITH PRIORITY NEEDS

After identifying priority needs, the district must ensure that the initiatives it implements both align with and address those needs. The initiatives must *respond* to a root cause identified through inquiry. Figure 4.1 provides a simple diagram that illustrates how the initiatives emerge from an identification of a priority need and root cause.

If a district identifies an achievement gap between male and female students in writing and decides to focus on addressing this need but simultaneously implements a new social studies curriculum, chances are good that neither area will improve as much as it would if it had full district support. If the district decided to align its resources behind the priority need of addressing the achievement gap in writing, then its initiatives would speak directly to that need and the corresponding root cause. When the district determines through data that the social studies curriculum is the priority need, then it can implement initiatives supporting social studies.

Simple in theory, this task is particularly challenging in practice. It requires diligently resisting engaging in opportunities that offer potential for learning and growth outside the priority area. While this may seem counterintuitive to districts—whose role exists in part to provide development opportunities to the professionals within its schools—it will dramatically enhance the efficacy of improvement efforts.

At Delaware Elementary School in Evansville, a narrow, directed focus yielded dramatic improvements in student learning. Resisting the initiative overload

FIGURE 4.1

CHRONOLOGY

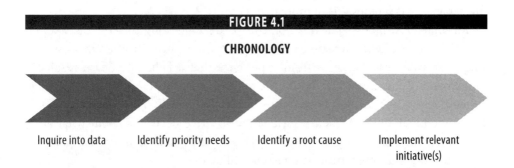

Inquire into data   Identify priority needs   Identify a root cause   Implement relevant initiative(s)

common in Title I schools, teachers and administrators focused on addressing student weaknesses in problem solving. Collectively, the faculty utilized collaborative time among teachers to implement instruction that promoted student skills in multistep problems, particularly through the Gradual Release of Responsibility.[3] The faculty's efforts, which protected time for teacher collaboration, resulted in double-digit math proficiency growth in all grades formally assessed. Math proficiency among third, fourth, and fifth graders increased by 10 percent, 29 percent, and 28 percent, respectively, in the course of one academic year. Just as a rising tide lifts all boats, addressing a root cause can yield improvements in related areas.

Concrete gains demonstrate the power of the work of CSI, in which the district's role is crucial. At the district level, leaders must ensure that what they expect of schools is both focused in scope and aligned with district and school needs. This process requires the DTT to thoughtfully limit the number of mandated initiatives or allow schools to choose which initiatives are most relevant to their needs. In a typical district, district leaders identify and mandate initiatives; within CSI, district leaders mandate the use of an inquiry cycle, shifting the decision power about needs and relevant initiatives to the school.

The partnership between the school and DTT provides a clear avenue for supporting alignment. In Evansville, the district lead interacts regularly with STTs to ensure that she is always aware of the priority needs that each school has identified. By keeping in close contact with school teams and staying informed about the work they are undertaking, the district lead is able to provide resources that align with the schools' focal areas. In addition, she can encourage connections among schools that are focusing on similar needs, magnifying alignment within the district as a whole, and building cohesiveness in the way the district does business. Building alignment among schools also fosters collaboration, idea sharing, and innovation, which in turn lead to changes in teaching practices and increases in student learning. Chapter 6 discusses this in more detail.

You may be wondering at this point if we are suggesting that the district and schools temporarily ignore some areas as part of their prioritization process. The simple answer: yes. We know from experience that a failure to do so results in implementing initiatives that have little or no impact on teaching and learning. When districts and schools use inquiry to identify priority needs, they can apply that intentional and informed prioritization to drive decisions about what areas receive attention and resources. Leaders then make calculated allocation of appropriate resources to those areas, and results will follow.

THE DISTRICT TRANSFORMATION TEAM'S ROLE IN ALIGNMENT

The DTT creates the model for the practice of alignment. In other words, if the district fails to value the alignment of initiatives—particularly at the top levels of the organization—schools will struggle to maintain a focus on high-priority needs. The DTT can create a working model of alignment by narrowing the focus at the district level, providing clarity, and creating a menu of options.

Narrowing the Focus at the District Level

Similar to the process at the school level, identifying high-priority needs at the district level will provide the starting point for narrowing the focus of district initiatives. A school may decide to devote its attention and resources to reducing the achievement gap between black and white students in math or to improving a specific skill required for proficiency in reading comprehension. It may decide to engage in improvement efforts in both areas. What the identification of these needs provides, however, is a barometer for screening initiatives within schools and the district. Once leaders have identified these areas of priority focus, they can more accurately assess the relevance of implementing initiatives.

Likely, this practice will involve "weeding the garden," in the words of Douglas Reeves. District leaders will need to eliminate some initiatives in order to provide adequate resources for others to flourish. Priority needs guide the decisions about which "weeds" to pull.[4]

Engaging in this practice at the district level will support this work in schools as well. Failing to create alignment at one level of the organization limits the effectiveness of alignment at other levels. For instance, if schools narrow their focus but simultaneously receive a wave of initiatives from the district, they will struggle to concentrate their resources appropriately. Likewise, if the district aligns its focus with priority needs but fails to support the school in engaging in a similar practice, dispersed improvement efforts will persist.

In addition to weeding the garden, alignment requires that districts and schools avoid the "flavor of the day" initiatives. General excitement or proven effectiveness cannot be the only requirements for district or school adoption of a practice or program. The DTT has a valuable role in this process, as it is in a unique position to understand schools' priority needs through its interaction in CSI. It may likely fall on the DTT members to be ongoing advocates for narrowing the focus and creating alignment.

Narrowing both the quantity and scope of initiatives supports alignment and strengthens each improvement area by concentrating the effort and energy it receives. There is something incredibly compelling—both intangibly and in practice—about walking into a building, asking any teacher what the school is focusing on improving that year, and receiving a similar response from each individual. The probability of making genuine improvements in teaching and learning increases dramatically when initiatives receive focused attention from a whole body of professionals.

In Portland, the process of engaging in CSI proved the value of narrowing the focus. To clarify its priorities and model a narrow, deep focus to schools, the district created a new school improvement plan (SIP). This new SIP reflected the language of the inquiry cycle (including each school's identification of a learner-centered problem, problem of practice, and instructional strategy). Whereas the district had previously required goals in every content area, the new SIP required a goal in only one content area, narrowing the focus for both the district and the schools.

A high school in Chandler experienced dramatic improvements in teaching and in student learning as a result of focusing on a high-priority need that it identified by engaging in the district inquiry cycle. The STT members led the entire staff of nearly two hundred teachers in protocols to examine teaching practices and student performance in all subject areas. They determined that students were least proficient in math—specifically, in manipulating fractions. Upon agreeing that fractions were *high leverage*—meaning that improving student understanding of fractions had the potential for improving many areas of math proficiency—school leaders and teachers explored their current instructional practices. Not surprisingly, they discovered that fractions—though a critical concept for mastery of many mathematical principles—were not consistently incorporated in non-math subjects. With this root cause and priority need identified, the whole faculty committed to modeling fractions within the context of various content areas. Math teachers provided additional support to teachers in preparation for instruction.

Strongly backing this school's work, the district leveraged its resources to offer support. It set up monthly training sessions, allocated money to hire substitutes so that teachers could spend time observing student work in action, and set aside time to collaborate. With access to these key district resources, the STT led the entire school in an effort to improve the teaching of fractions—in all subjects and across all grade levels. History teachers supported the effort by assigning a fraction of a book to be read for homework. English teachers followed suit and took every opportunity to discuss parts of the whole in daily lessons. This schoolwide effort resulted in a 15 percent growth in proficiency in the fractions strand and a 10 percent growth in overall math proficiency in the course of one year.

The success Chandler experienced exemplifies the impact of identifying priority needs and a narrow entry point for addressing each one. Focusing on fractions contributed not only to gains within this subcontent area, but also to substantial gains in math overall. The rising tide in one area ultimately lifted all boats in the water.

Providing Clarity

While schools will identify their own school-specific priority needs, the district should clarify how initiatives align with priority needs at both school and district levels. The DTT must first create clarity among its own members about the alignment of initiatives before it can support schools in developing a parallel understanding.

In Portland, district personnel created specific opportunities to explore how the simultaneous implementations of Response to Intervention (RtI) and the Data Wise Improvement Process (their identified data-driven inquiry cycle) aligned with each other, and with the districtwide focus on using data to make informed decisions.[5] Several individuals at the district level met to identify areas in which RtI and Data Wise overlapped. This required a deep understanding of the essential elements and purposes of each process. From there, the district was able to align language to embed the two processes together, placing RtI within the Data Wise model. Such clarity informed the team's ability to develop a timeline that aligned both processes. With their shared understanding, the DTT members were equipped to support similar clarity among the schools in the district.

The DTT can be a powerful impetus for aligning initiatives within the district. In Evansville, the district identifies data-driven inquiry and decision making as "the Evansville way," and DTT members use their current inquiry cycle (the Data Wise Improvement Process) as the litmus test for new initiatives. When the team was considering whether to implement Instructional Rounds—a process to collect and analyze instructional practice through classroom observations—it brought in an independent consultant. Soon, the DTT realized that this new process diverged from current improvement efforts. Instead of pursuing the implementation of Instructional Rounds as a separate initiative, it created a process for classroom peer observations that fit into its existing inquiry process. Adapting valuable pieces of the Instructional Rounds model, the team developed a method for collecting classroom-level data that aligned with "the Evansville way." Even through identifying this phrase and its corresponding meaning, the DTT set the stage for clear communication to schools throughout the district. Faculty members across the district now understand that data collection and inquiry are the standard modes of operation in the Evansville Vanderburgh School Corporation.

The district transformation team plays a critical role within the process of alignment. In addition to encouraging a narrow focus on high-priority needs (and streamlining corresponding initiatives), the DTT must develop and instill a vision for improvement work districtwide. This team will have a unique perspective, informed by its involvement with school teams throughout CSI. As the individuals at the district level who best understand the work of inquiry, the DTT bears a responsibility to apply this knowledge and perspective to its work as it aligns initiatives with high-priority needs.

Creating and Providing a Menu of Options

Traditionally, districts expect schools to engage in a variety of districtwide initiatives. In a typical district, this often generates a handful of committees within each school building that work separately and simultaneously to implement these top-down initiatives, producing disconnected change efforts. In contrast, CSI recommends that the DTT instead create and provide a menu of options to schools. Through their chosen inquiry cycle, schools will identify school-specific needs and can then use the inquiry process to select relevant district support for their initiatives.

For example, in their third year of engaging schools in inquiry-based improvement, district leaders in Evansville were united in building a districtwide culture that centered on inquiry and identifying priority needs at both the district and school levels. The DTT determined that it could support schools in narrowing their focus by creating a menu of professional development options for them. The team realized that, in order for improvement efforts to be most effective, schools should be allowed to select only those offerings that would directly support the priority needs that they had identified as part of the inquiry process. By letting them prioritize their own needs, district leaders empowered schools to more effectively address teaching and learning.

Having a menu of choices does not absolve schools of the expectation that they are engaging in ongoing inquiry and improvement efforts. While participating in CSI, the district will likely mandate some initiatives; however, instead of expressing district thinking, the initiatives will support the school-level inquiry cycle. In Evansville, the district mandates an inquiry process, sending a clear message that inquiry is "the way we do business." Recognizing a districtwide achievement gap, the district in Portland requires a focus on equity. From these starting points, districts can then offer choices to schools. Rather than mandating schools' participation in a plethora of simultaneous improvement efforts, districts simply require that schools address the root causes of their priority needs in a meaningful way, and in doing so, leverage the partnership with the district.

CONCLUSION

While alignment has traditionally entailed linking initiatives to one another, Collaborative School Improvement defines alignment as prioritizing data-identified needs, determining narrow entry points for addressing each, and mapping resources to those needs. As we've seen in districts across the country, failing to engage in this process results in dispersed improvement efforts, which lack the power to drive meaningful changes in teaching and learning. When teachers and school and district leaders identify their priority needs, and then take time to explore and understand them deeply, they can make informed decisions about which initiatives are most relevant to their improvement efforts.

■

TAKEAWAYS

- *We cannot boil the ocean: focusing on a high-priority need is more effective than working with various initiatives simultaneously.* Experience has demonstrated that attempting to address myriad needs at the same time overdraws resources, depriving all initiatives of the attention they need for effective implementation, and minimizing improvements in teaching and student learning. Instead, we must prioritize our needs through a holistic examination of data, narrowing our focus so that our efforts can drive meaningful improvements in student outcomes.

- *Shooting in the dark isn't good target practice: effective improvement efforts begin with a narrow entry point, identified through inquiry.* When we deeply explore student learning, we are equipped to identify an area—in direct response to a root cause—on which to focus our efforts. This process helps us truly understand student needs and implement a solution that directly addresses them. Common practices in schools tend to focus on implementing solutions before deeply understanding problems, which is akin to shooting in the dark: it commonly fails to make lasting changes because it misses the target.

- *Grease the squeakiest wheel: the district transformation team must create the vision and establish the model for narrowing the focus on the highest priority needs.* If the district fails to align its priorities (and allocate resources) with its greatest needs, schools will struggle to do the same. When the district actively partners with schools in supporting this practice, it models how narrowing the focus is both possible and essential.

CHAPTER 5

Lead with Purpose

Redefining District Leadership for CSI

During a district meeting in Chandler, leaders reflect on their significant investments in school improvement over the last decade, including increasing the professional development (PD) offerings in topics such as leadership, assessment, and data analysis. During a brainstorming session, these leaders wonder out loud about how they could take a more prominent role in school improvement. "I feel like I could do more than simply offering PD—I know many things about school improvement. I realize that I'm not in school buildings all the time, but I want schools to respect what I can offer as a leader." Others nod, acknowledging the fragile balance between leading and supporting. Believing in the need for school-level decision making, one speaks up, "Let's remember that while we all want to take a stronger role in school improvement, we can't create top-down initiatives. If teachers don't feel ownership, nothing else we do will matter."

THE PROBLEM

In this age of high expectations, districts are invested in leading school improvements. In the past, however, individual schools shouldered much of the challenge of improving teaching and student learning outcomes within their buildings. As we've discussed in earlier chapters, schools were unsure how to communicate with districts and unclear about the roles each of them should play in the school improvement process. But going it alone brings only a fraction of available resources and wisdom to the table. Research shows that without leadership and involvement from the district office, reform efforts that focus on supporting teaching and learning improvements will not be realized at scale.[1] If we expect improvement efforts to ultimately lead to increases in student learning, schools need to partner with the district transformation team. Guided by a shared vision, this team of district leaders will work directly with school transformation teams to put the vision into practice.

REDEFINING DISTRICT LEADERSHIP FOR SCHOOL IMPROVEMENT

Collaborative School Improvement calls for enacting changes and demystifying the role of the DTT as leaders in school improvement—a role that supersedes the traditional roles of district leaders and necessitates the implementation of the practices outlined in this book. In our work with districts in CSI, we have identified seven key practices that characterize effective DTTs:

1. Creating and maintaining a vision
2. Modeling inquiry
3. Modeling how to effectively function as a team
4. Teaching the required skills
5. Providing relevant resources
6. Setting high expectations
7. Providing regular and thoughtful feedback

Effective leaders are key to large-scale, sustainable education reform.[2] For CSI practices to be effectively implemented across a district, leaders at the district level—from the superintendent to the department heads—must be prepared to change the district's existing leadership structures and adopt new roles. In these new roles, district leaders (and particularly the DTT) will guide and encourage their partners—the STTs—in making decisions about improvement at the school level. When STTs receive this support, they develop a deeper understanding of the value the district brings to the table.

Creating and Maintaining the Vision

To implement sustainable and scalable initiatives that meet their highest-priority needs, district leaders need a solid plan—a long-term vision for what they want to accomplish and what methods will be most successful. Naming this districtwide vision builds a feeling of trust, collaboration, and a mutual sense of responsibility for success among all participants in CSI. The DTT is responsible for relaying this plan to school leaders and teachers and building momentum around it.

At least three elements of the vision you create are essential. First, district teams should indicate that the ultimate outcome of the work is increased student learning. This enhancement in student learning is generated, of course, through improvements in teaching. Second, inquiry is the new way of identifying needs and creating action plans. And, finally, the district needs to signal that its role is one of active partner for school improvement. This partnership will start with the district embodying new practices, the purpose of which is to lead and support schools through school improvement.

Evansville exemplified the practice of taking the essential elements and making the vision its own. Committed to building a transparent culture of partnership and inquiry, the DTT developed and communicated a vision for a districtwide culture of inquiry, which it called "the Evansville way." This made the vision less about someone else's model (such as the chosen inquiry cycle or CSI) and more about the district's tailored application of the work.

Modeling Inquiry

Effective leaders talk the talk *and* walk the walk. The DTT must model what it is asking schools to do. In CSI, this requires leaders to function effectively as a team and model the practice of using inquiry to identify needs.

As wisely noted by Mohandas Gandhi, "An ounce of practice is worth more than tons of preaching." By modeling the work rather than just talking about it, the DTT is better equipped to lead schools in inquiry-based decision making. When STTs see the DTT modeling elements of the inquiry process, they become more confident in the districtwide vision and are more likely to feel ownership over the process at their schools. When modeling the inquiry cycle, the DTT should pay close attention to the essential elements outlined in box 5.1 (they are defined in chapter 1).

In Chandler, the DTT modeled the effective use of inquiry to identify and subsequently address needs. To begin, the DTT attended monthly inquiry training sessions and used inquiry to identify specific needs in the district. For instance, by looking at data and engaging in conversations with STTs, the district identified a substantial hole in its current assessments. This turned out to be a high-priority need: the assessment reports that the district had been supplying were not providing the information that schools needed; as a result, many schools were not even

---

BOX 5.1

ESSENTIAL ELEMENTS OF THE INQUIRY CYCLE

- Step-by-step process
- A focus on the instructional core
- A focus on narrow, concrete problems and solutions that address a root cause
- An expanded definition of data
- The use of protocols and norms
- Whole-staff decision making
- Progress monitoring

---

looking at the reports. With this inquiry-generated realization in mind, the DTT collaboratively adjusted its current assessment reports. These useful reports meant that teachers had the data they needed in their hands when they needed it—soon enough to affect instruction and improve their students' learning.

By modeling the use of inquiry to identify a narrow, concrete problem, the DTT sent a clear message to schools that the district's vision of inquiry-based improvement was something that it, too, would work to implement. In addition, the DTT gained valuable insight about the inquiry process itself, which it could use to support STTs throughout the inquiry cycle. Participating schools valued the district's perspective even more because of the relevance of the DTT's feedback and support.

Inquiry is essential to results-based, organic planning. Modeling inquiry gives the DTT concrete tools for meeting the goals and expectations outlined in the district vision for CSI. To build a culture of inquiry within the district, the DTT must be responsive and make plans that directly address the school needs. Planning this way empowers district and school transformation teams to address needs as they arise and to help schools realize the shared district vision.

Modeling How to Effectively Function as a Team

One of the DTT's core roles is to explicitly model how to function efficiently and engage effectively in inquiry. We view *explicit* modeling as different from traditional modeling. Explicit modeling seeks opportunities to demonstrate vulnerability and progress to the district as a whole. The DTT's job is not to be quiet about its struggles or successes.

While the subject of teaming at the school level is discussed in detail in chapter 3, this section describes how the DTT leads districtwide implementation of CSI by modeling how to:

- Bring together diverse members of district leadership to collaborate and contribute to CSI
- Engage in facilitative leadership to show school teams how shared leadership can best meet the needs of school improvement efforts
- Build soft skills, including effective collaboration

Bring together diverse individuals to collaborate and contribute to CSI

The members of school transformation teams are likely to be as diverse as the members of the district transformation team—they represent a wide range of skill sets, knowledge, and abilities, but they must learn to function efficiently together. Diverse teams can generate better thinking and creative outcomes when faced with challenges. By modeling the effective team practices described in chapter 3, the DTT immediately establishes that these practices are an essential component of school improvement.

Engage in facilitative leadership

By employing facilitative leadership, transformation teams will benefit from the sense of collaboration and coherence that emerges when all stakeholders feel collective ownership for leading the work. By engaging in collaborative work, team members can tap into their individual strengths and make the best use of the skills and knowledge that each person brings to the table.

Build soft skills

Finally, the DTT will help STTs function more effectively by modeling soft skills that are integral to the practices of CSI. Discussed in greater detail in chapter 3, these skills include using time effectively, collaborating, and developing coherence. Through emphasizing the importance of developing these soft skills, the DTT sends a clear message that this skill set is essential to its new way of doing business.

Teaching the Skills

In Chandler, eleven school transformation teams arrived at the district office to participate in Data Wise Improvement Process training.[3] This first meeting was the kickoff for a yearlong commitment from the schools to engage in data-driven decision making. This session covered the basics of the inquiry cycle that the DTT had selected. Early on, participants expressed apprehension about the dramatic cultural shifts required to implement the Data Wise Improvement Process. But as the DTT explained the training and support accompanying the process, teams developed confidence in their ability to act as leaders and facilitators of the work. Following the first training session, a majority of the participants expressed confidence in being able to lead their schools in the process (a percentage that continued to grow throughout the first year of implementation). That's pretty impressive, considering that the Data Wise Improvement Process was a major shift from the current mode of doing business for these STTs.

Chandler's experience demonstrates the role that the DTT plays in leading schools through CSI. After selecting an inquiry cycle and the participating schools for the first cohort, the DTT leveraged outside experts in data-driven inquiry to provide Data Wise Improvement Process training. Buying books and expecting spontaneous improvements is not enough. The district needs to practice, model, and teach the skills.

Many variables affect the way that districts choose to lead schools in CSI. Some districts (like Chandler) elect to use an outside expert to lead the work in the initial years of implementation. Other districts decide to team up with internal experts to provide the training that STTs need. Table 5.1 lists some of the possibilities that districts should explore when considering how to best lead STTs. Portland, in collaboration with the Nike School Innovation Fund, determined that teacher development could be enhanced and student achievement increased if the DTT provided training with the support of an outside expert. For more information about utilizing external support, see chapter 7.

Using data

As a result of the No Child Left Behind Act (NCLB) in 2001, most districts in the U.S. have systems in place for storing the vast amount of data that they regularly collect. These systems are, in essence, treasure troves of information for improving teaching and learning districtwide. In order for schools to use this data to make decisions, they need to have easy access to it, and they need to understand what it

TABLE 5.1

OPTIONS FOR LEADING SCHOOL TRANSFORMATION TEAMS IN INQUIRY TRAINING

District led	Outside support
▪ Provide book studies (focusing on school improvement) ▪ Leverage internal experts to lead training sessions	▪ Offer training sessions led by outside provider ▪ Partner with outside provider to lead training sessions ▪ Partner with other experts to lead training sessions (e.g., neighboring districts that have successfully implemented the process in their schools)

means. Simply put, if schools can't access the data, they can't use it. If they can get to it but don't know what it indicates, they can't use it either. In many cases, preparing schools to access and comprehend data requires professional development and ongoing support from assessment experts within the district.

Inquiry requires the use of data to inform decision making, and provides schools with the tools to "aim" before "firing." Districts must provide assessment literacy training so that teams are adequately prepared to analyze and understand data on a regular basis.

As an example, the DTT in Chandler invited an internal expert to teach the STTs about accessing data and using it to identify root-cause problems related to teaching and learning. She provided teams with quick-start guides to aid them in the future, and offered her assistance to all schools as they engaged in data-driven inquiry.

PROVIDING RELEVANT RESOURCES

By customizing support *in response to* an individual school's needs, districts are more likely to provide relevant and useful resources. Rather than approaching their role as leaders from the top down, DTT members take responsibility for providing school-specific support and resources. In Evansville, where the DTT regularly provided the same resources to all schools, this shift was eye opening. Depending on their status in the inquiry process, schools needed different support from the district: some requested PD to address root causes of priority needs; some needed support in generating action items based on the information returned by the district assessment reports; and others appealed for financial assistance to hire substitute teachers so that teachers could spend time observing peers in order to collaborate more effectively. By giving schools support that directly related to their identified needs—and by giving them the autonomy to determine what these needs were—the DTT empowered its schools to succeed in their inquiry processes.

The transformation team at one elementary school in Portland discovered through inquiry how it could best support teachers in their work. Since this school was focusing on increasing writing proficiency for male students, the transformation team, teachers, and staff determined that holding monthly writing workshops featuring local male writers would provide insight into the minds of male writers. The STT approached the DTT and submitted a proposal to use its PD time and money to provide these workshops for teachers. The district supported these specific needs, offered expertise to inform one of the sessions, and was thrilled to see in the medium-term data that its PD investment led to substantial gains in writing proficiency for the focus subgroup.

The DTT in Portland took pride in collaborating with schools to effectively infuse district resources into high-priority needs that addressed the instructional core. Shifting its traditional approach to providing professional development, it based all decisions regarding PD on school-specific needs that had been identified through data-driven inquiry.[4]

Time and funding

CSI requires that time be set aside for collaborative teamwork—both within schools and across the district. Chapter 3 covers this topic in detail, and highlights the benefits and challenges of generating the time to focus on inquiry for the purpose of improving teaching and learning. School transformation teams must be given time to attend training sessions, to engage in inquiry outside of training sessions, and to engage their staff in inquiry at their schools. In addition, STT members and staff will need time to look more deeply into student data and observe practice.

Districts can fund this time in a number of ways. For many districts that we have assisted, the option of funding release time is most feasible—teachers' classes are covered while training and planning take place. Some districts and schools prefer to limit the hours that teachers are away from their classrooms, so they hold training sessions during noncontract hours, offering pay to participating teachers for their time. This approach alleviates the need for substitute teachers and reduces the amount of instructional time lost, but requires a larger overall time commitment from teachers. In Portland, district leaders designated time for whole-staff, inquiry-based collaborative work during monthly late-start time slots. As a result, all teachers were able to take part without requiring extra pay, and no instructional time was lost.

Relevant professional development

The old saying, "if you always do what you've always done, you'll always get what you've always gotten," holds true in the realm of professional development. If leaders work diligently to implement CSI across the district but continue to provide PD in the same way that they always have, they will not see the changes in teaching and learning that they expect. CSI requires districts to rethink PD, which will likely be a struggle for some districts where "old system structures do not easily support new approaches to PD."[5]

First, teachers must receive more than one-stop PD, which nets improvements in teaching that are marginal at best. Instead of offering flavor-of-the-month topics, the DTT must offer relevant, timely PD that responds to needs identified through inquiry. Many districts seek outside experts to aid them in providing necessary support. By restructuring PD opportunities, districts can successfully support teachers in building knowledge and skills that will contribute to gains in student achievement.[6] Table 5.2 outlines what these shifts in PD might look like.

Setting High Expectations

In classrooms, high expectations regularly lead to high performance, and low expectations frequently result in low performance. Where teachers set high expectations, they are transparent, they monitor outcomes of student performance, and they accept nothing less than the best. The DTT must send a clear message to schools that CSI is not "just another thing" by setting high expectations that apply to the outcomes as well as to the process of data-driven inquiry. Similarly, the team must be completely transparent and focus its expectations on the vision of CSI in these areas:

- Implementing the inquiry cycle with fidelity
- Making changes to instruction that focus on the instructional core
- Increasing student learning

TABLE 5.2

PROFESSIONAL DEVELOPMENT BEFORE AND DURING CSI

Before CSI	During CSI
Districts provided "generic" professional development offerings to all teachers.	Districts provide relevant PD opportunities in response to needs identified by schools through the inquiry process.
Districts offered one-time PD sessions.	PD offerings are supplemented with ongoing training.
Resources were not used in the most effective ways to improve instruction.	Resources, offered in direct response to schools' needs, are leveraged to most effectively impact instruction.
PD offerings were a result of someone in the district office attending a conference and bringing "the next great thing" back to the district.	PD offerings are research-based and offered for the purpose of building capacity for high-quality instruction that focuses on the instructional core.
Districts passed down PD opportunities to schools without collaborating with the schools to identify their needs.	The district transformation team works with school transformation teams to provide teachers with the PD that they need.

While our examples (in table 5.3) are not intended to provide a comprehensive picture of setting high expectations in each of these areas, they should give you an idea of how these expectations might look in practice.

Providing Regular and Thoughtful Feedback

Research shows that teacher feedback to students is more "strongly and consistently related to achievement than any other teaching behavior."[7] We have found the same to be true in the DTT's role to lead and support schools: the district transformation team should provide regular and thoughtful feedback to STTs.

To provide knowledgeable feedback, the DTT must review evidence for how each STT's goals have or have not been met. Rather than evaluating the STTs, the DTT uses evidence to communicate objectively and descriptively about how teams can alter their plans to reach their goals. Consider how the following district leaders examined evidence to generate useful feedback.

Having just received submissions from school teams outlining midyear gains in student learning, the DTT began its meeting by reiterating its vision of

TABLE 5.3

SETTING HIGH EXPECTATIONS

Area of high expectations	Example
Implementing the inquiry cycle with fidelity	Schools in Chandler were required to implement every step in the inquiry cycle that the district chose to drive improvement efforts. As a way of maintaining this expectation, the district transformation team checked in with school transformation teams on a regular basis. Data Wise training was hyperfocused on helping teams learn the process step by step, so that they would be able to implement it with fidelity the first time around and in coming years. Together with the outside provider, district leaders recognized that, though this approach to teaching the steps was slow-going at times, it accomplished the priority goal of providing teams with a deep understanding of the process.
Making changes to instruction that focus on the instructional core	School transformation teams in Portland were required to implement changes in instruction that focused on the instructional core, as opposed to choosing strategies that focused solely on either teaching practices or student learning. These instructional changes were listed in schools' improvement plans, and implementation indicators were included to show understanding of both the core strategies and their desired outcomes for student learning once those strategies were implemented.
Increasing student learning	In Evansville, the district transformation team's high expectations for schools to increase student learning were clear from the day that the district started engaging in data-driven inquiry. The district transformation team set the expectation that all schools would see gains in student learning, and that the DDT would share these gains at the schools and across the district at regular intervals. To facilitate this, the transformation team required each school to create and maintain a medium-term data display that clearly showed student performance in its area of focus. These displays were posted in places around the schools where all teachers and staff could see them, and they were also shared at quarterly district meetings.

inquiry-based improvement and reviewing what each school's goals were for the year. The team then looked at the progress monitoring plans one by one, noting goals for student achievement growth as well as plans to assess students with short-, medium-, and long-term measures. It examined the data that schools had provided to show student learning. While there was evidence that some schools were progressing toward their goals, others seemed to be at a standstill. For these schools, the DTT wrote specific recommendations and feedback on the plans that they had submitted.

By basing its feedback to schools on evidence, garnered by looking at the nitty-gritty details of each school's plans, the DTT is able to offer relevant ideas and solutions that directly respond to the schools' needs. Additionally, STTs will best be able to implement feedback that provides specific and actionable recommendations. The feedback is meant as a resource, not an evaluation, and should be communicated with this in mind.

Districts Before and During CSI

On the whole, school districts look different once they have implemented CSI. The shifts that lead to long-term, scalable improvement are especially noticeable in leadership at the district level. Table 5.4 provides a snapshot of how some of these changes might look in your district, of course depending on where you are when you start CSI.

CONCLUSION

For districts to successfully implement the practices of Collaborative School Improvement, they must establish a team of leaders (the DTT) that will effectively support schools by creating and maintaining a vision, modeling the inquiry work, teaching the required skills, providing relevant resources, setting high expectations, and providing regular and thoughtful feedback. Collectively, these practices direct the roles of the district within CSI.

TABLE 5.4

DISTRICT LEADERSHIP BEFORE AND DURING CSI

Before CSI	During CSI
Roles are ambiguous.	Roles are clearly defined (supported by the formation of a district transformation team).
Lack of individuals being explicitly named to lead district improvement efforts inhibits scalable school improvement efforts.	Effective leaders serve on the DTT, contributing to the success of scalable school improvement efforts.
Leaders are hyperfocused on day-to-day central office operations.	The DTT is focused on providing support to schools that will lead to improvement districtwide.
Leaders and schools have a top-down relationship.	Partnerships are formed between leaders (the DTT) and school transformation teams.
Leaders don't have a vision for what *school improvement* means in the district.	Leaders clearly state the vision of CSI and develop a shared vision with all stakeholders.
Improvement efforts lack focus.	Improvement efforts focus on a long-term commitment to building a culture of inquiry that results in changes in teaching and gains in student learning.
Leaders have a "do as I say" leadership style.	DTT members "walk the walk"—modeling the use of inquiry and effective team practices.
Leadership is typically transactional, giving complete autonomy to district leaders.	Facilitative leadership ensures that all stakeholders are invested and contributing.
Leaders use a blanket approach to provide resources—everyone gets everything.	The DTT provides relevant resources to schools in response to the needs the schools have identified through inquiry.
Professional development is treated as "one size fits all."	PD is customized to meet schools' needs (and schools are given the autonomy to choose what is best for them).
The Pygmalion effect applies—low expectations are likely to yield low outcomes.	High expectations for all schools are more likely to lead to high outcomes.
Leaders provide little or no feedback to schools.	The DTT gives regular, thoughtful feedback—directly related to the vision—to all schools.

■

TAKEAWAYS

- *Under new management: a new definition of leadership is essential to the success of districtwide, scalable school improvement efforts.* This leadership centers on creating and maintaining a vision, modeling the inquiry work, teaching the required skills, providing relevant resources, setting high expectations, and providing regular and thoughtful feedback. By intentionally engaging with schools, the district gains perspective that is essential to effectively supporting the work of inquiry-based school improvement in each building.

- *How can we help? CSI reframes the traditional relationship between the district and schools within the area of improvement efforts.* Rather than initiating specific plans or initiatives from the top down, districts become adaptive and responsive to the priority needs that schools identify. Effectively implementing this shift requires clear communication with schools about the expectations of and accountability for improvement efforts at all levels of the organization.

- *Road work ahead: changes in district leadership patterns are necessary for building an effective partnership between districts and the schools they serve.* If a district is truly committed to building a culture of inquiry, where schools have the capacity to identify and address school-specific needs and their root causes, changes in the district's current way of doing business are necessary.

CHAPTER 6

Connect Teams

Creating Opportunities for Celebrating
and Sharing Best Practices

In Evansville, Director of Professional Development Emily Smith-McCormick sat behind her desk and contemplated the differences among schools in her district. From the reports in her hand, she could see that while some schools were thriving, others were not experiencing the same success. Having worked alongside school leaders, she was keenly aware that pockets of excellence existed across the district—even small pockets of success shone within what she considered less successful schools. Wouldn't it be handy, Emily mused, if successful school transformation teams could work with the others, collaborating to share functional techniques? What would it take to make that happen? The district didn't offer any protocol or defined opportunities for sharing successful techniques, and clearly the schools were not spontaneously collaborating with one another to replicate success. Emily knew there had to be a way for the district to identify best practices and facilitate their transfer to other schools. It was simply logical for the district to play that role. Optimistically, Emily began developing strategies to initiate this kind of cross-school collaboration.

THE PROBLEM

All educators want to offer the best instruction for their students. That's a blanket assertion, but we haven't yet met an educator who isn't committed to improving student learning. The problem educators face is that no one has a perfect method that works for every teacher and every student. Often, individual teachers and administrators develop innovations that work for a year or two, and you'd think that their techniques would spread like wildfire . . . but they don't. Why not? Because their classrooms and offices have doors. District leaders, school administrators, and teachers rarely walk through one another's doors and learn from their colleagues. They miss crucial opportunities to cultivate shared expertise and collaborate on innovations—to compare notes, in essence. Teachers, schools, and district leaders have a lot on their plates, so facilitating such connections is rarely a top priority. As a result, innovative ideas that individual schools successfully implement generally go unshared districtwide.

Emily and her team uncovered this piece of the puzzle as they looked at the current insufficient practices for cross-team collaboration. After doing some serious research, Emily's team found that schools within the district spent hours re-creating strategies and teaching practices that had already been optimized by others—sometimes even by people within the same schools. Emily's team recognized the obvious: if school leaders and teachers could be on the same page strategically, they could pool their efforts rather than clearing the same forest again and again. In addition, her team found that school leaders, transformation teams, and teachers were rarely reaching out to the district for much-needed assistance because they felt some confusion about the district's role in supporting school improvement. The fact that isolated individuals were engaging in the work of school improvement without collaboration or district support may seem absurd, but, unfortunately, in districts across the country, it is often the norm.[1]

THE IMPACT OF CONNECTING

Emily Smith-McCormick and her team developed a plan to facilitate consistent collaboration toward the common goal of improving teaching and learning. Leveraging her weight as the district's Director of Professional Development, Emily put the plan into play, encouraging team conversations about collaboration. Over the next eighteen months, she saw positive changes in districtwide culture. Evidence showed that individuals were building upon the ideas and innovations that their peers were sharing with them, and that the culture of collaboration was thriving. With district support, schools in Evansville developed the habit of actively seeking input from their colleagues, incorporating useful ideas, and celebrating the successes that they were experiencing. Through their collaboration, the district as a whole gained insight into best practices and innovations in education—and these insights led to notable increases in student learning.

Impact on School Transformation Teams

During this process, transformation teams at all of the schools in the Evansville Vanderburgh School Corporation recognized the value of regularly discussing their successes and talking through the challenges they faced. As transformation teams in Evansville began collecting medium-term data to track progress, Emily realized that they could benefit from examples of the practice in action. Having heard about a data-collection tool that team members at Cynthia Heights Elementary School (CHES) created to show student gains in writing, Emily approached the school transformation team—which was a pocket of excellence in the district—and asked it to share its idea at a districtwide training meeting.

To ensure this school's success, Emily invited the district's outside experts to support the CHES team as it presented its data-collection tool to other teams at a training session. The outside experts helped the team create a tight agenda (see box 6.1) for the day of the presentation, ensuring that it shared sufficient content and detail to enable other schools to replicate its success.

As the transformation team members from CHES stood before their colleagues and enthusiastically presented their medium-term data-collection tool, they explained that they had collaborated with staff members from multiple grade levels to create a simple graphical display showing the gains in student writing. The team discussed how its classroom-based, medium-term data-collection tool involved students and kept them aware of their own progress. To represent their scores on weekly writing prompts, students placed a sticker on one of the petals on a flower chart. These graphic displays reminded both the teachers and the students of their hard work, and visually tracked progress toward their goal. Because their tool was flexible, teachers had some autonomy in how they would use it in their classrooms—some decided to post the flower charts on the walls of their rooms, while others kept them in a notebook.

CHES team members discussed their success with the flower charts and played a short video about the data-collection process in action that showed students walking proudly to the flower patch displayed on the classroom wall and placing stickers on the flowers to indicate their scores. Illustrating the students' excitement, the engaging video motivated other schools to develop their own data-collection tools.

BOX 6.1

CROSS-SCHOOL SHARING AGENDA

3:00–3:05 Introduce the tool

- Why we created a tool for collecting classroom data

3:05–3:10 Discuss the importance of collaboration

- Explain the process that we went through with our staff as we developed the tool

3:10–3:15 Implementation/logistics

- How do we use the tool?
- Who uses the tool?
- How flexible is the tool?

3:15–3:20 Practicality

- How does the tool meet our needs?

3:20–3:30 Q&A

Source: Evansville Vanderburgh School Corporation, Evansville, Indiana

---

Before the team from Cynthia Heights Elementary could even wrap up its presentation, other teams were discussing how they could adapt the tool for their own schools. Thrilled with the response from their colleagues, the CHES team enjoyed listening to others from across the district plan to implement a data-collection method inspired by its tool. The CHES team's idea was literally going to change the way that dozens of schools approached the task of collecting medium-term data.

Zooming out for a minute, we can see how this moment exemplifies Emily Smith-McCormick's efforts to draw schools together in sharing successful practices: she identified a pocket of excellence and facilitated collaboration so that each school in her district could benefit from one school's innovation. This presentation helped teams in Evansville that were struggling with the challenge of collecting medium-term data. For these teams, the idea of adding something new to their already full daily regimen felt daunting. Having a chance to connect with colleagues throughout the district reminded them that they were not going through the process alone.

Seeing other teams engage in productive work demystified the team structure, and served as a catalyst for change in those schools that might otherwise have been reluctant to participate.

Emily's team realized that information shared between school teams was much more likely to stick than was information from the district. Like a child who whole-heartedly takes advice from his older brother (although his parents have offered the same advice on multiple occasions), school teams are more likely to internalize the things they learn directly from their peers. After sharing their idea and interacting with peers who encouraged them to think about scaling it up, the team members from Cynthia Heights decided to expand their classroom-based data-collection tool to help display data schoolwide. They created a single large flower and exhibited it within the building where everyone could see it. The stickers on the petals now represented classroom averages, thereby allowing teachers and students to track classroom gains in student learning.

After tasting success with the CHES team's presentation and the district's new peer-influenced enthusiasm for data-collection tools, Emily and her team decided to start a larger conversation about peer observation in Evansville. They proposed that having teachers spend time in one another's classrooms would generate team conversations about how school improvement actually happens. Classrooms are where the rubber meets the road—where theory turns into practice, and practice gets results. Some transformation teams expressed concern over time constraints and teacher anxiety about peer observation. Teachers from various teams admitted they were worried that their colleagues might view the observations as evaluations, rather than as opportunities to collect useful data.

To dispel these fears, the district again harnessed a "pocket of success" example and asked Delaware Elementary School faculty members to share stories about the successes they had experienced with peer observation at their school. At a training session, teachers from Delaware shared what the process looked like at their school, and presented it in a way that made it seem manageable (and far less threatening) to other school teams. They displayed their actual templates for collecting data during observations and made them available for other schools to adapt. Concerned school teams had the opportunity to ask the Delaware Elementary School team how it managed time constraints and teacher anxiety, and the discussions that followed offered further insight into the process.

School teams that were once hesitant to engage in peer observations became excited to do the work, commenting, "So that's what they meant by peer observation," and "Hey—we can do that at our school!" Chalk up another point for Emily's work in bringing teams together: one school's successful methods were now available for districtwide use. And districtwide use meant that pockets of success could become districtwide gains.

As Emily learned firsthand, connecting with other STTs allows schools to learn from one another, grow ideas together, and build a sense of community within the district. Gathering on a regular basis forms a sort of soft accountability within and among teams: they are much more likely to plan thoughtfully and come prepared with questions when they know that they are working as part of a larger group. Individual teams begin to hold themselves to a higher standard, knowing that the other teams within their district are working hard in the process of transforming teaching and learning.

Impact on District Transformation Teams

As teams in Chandler, Arizona, considered the current district assessments, they realized that they weren't measuring student growth or providing standard-specific data. Hoping to remove obstacles, the DTT set out to learn more about the problems that school teams had with existing assessments.

To accomplish this, the district team created a list of questions and allocated time at a training session for conversations about what the school teams wanted from district assessments. School teams talked with the district about what they felt was missing and made concrete recommendations about what would be most useful for their schools.

In this process, the district team also identified two major concerns that it would have missed had it not taken the time to connect with the school teams. First, it pinpointed the need for assessments that contained open-ended questions (which would provide greater insight into students' understanding). Second, it discovered that teachers needed access to assessments so that they could identify specific test questions that their students struggled with most often. Having access to this data would help teachers understand precisely what students knew about each concept addressed on the test. These two things—which might seem small on the surface—became the catalyst for district leaders to revise the assessments the district provided. By taking the time to connect, the district team learned more about the schools' specific needs, and its role in meeting these needs became clear.

Making meaningful connections also gives the district team insight into the progress patterns in individual schools. In Evansville, the district team gathered valuable information about which pitfalls were common across the district, and which struggles were isolated to individual schools. Having already experienced successful cross-school connection, the Evansville transformation team quickly identified a plan for providing partner teams to schools that needed a boost. In addition, the Evansville team effectively leveraged its outside expert to fill in any gaps.

Impact on the District as a Whole

In Evansville, transformation teams representing every school in the district work together to effect change in both teaching and learning. As a result of connecting and sharing, a districtwide culture emerged—now known as "the Evansville way." Teams are no longer just "doing Data Wise"; rather, district leaders, school administrators, and teachers are on the same page because they have been taught a new way of doing business as usual.[2] A culture of inquiry and collaboration is the norm: schools now regularly rely on one another to build upon ideas and share innovations. District leaders, principals, and teachers use shared language and have established a framework for how schools will examine teaching and learning. Faculty members use protocols consistently and effectively, attending to team-created group norms.

Districtwide changes occur in places like Evansville because of the frequent and consistent opportunities for school and district teams to come together and learn from the education experts who are working in their own backyard. Participating in this new way of doing business builds enthusiasm at all levels. Teachers are energized by the support that they receive both from their colleagues and district leaders. Schools like Cynthia Heights Elementary recognize positive changes that result from their efforts. District leaders witness the prospect of long-term changes unfolding. Following attendance at a cohort Data Wise training session, a school board member in Chandler commented on his newfound faith that the district and schools had the capacity to lead improvement efforts; his excitement about the work opened doors for future support from the board.

PROVIDING OPPORTUNITIES TO SHARE INNOVATION AND IDEAS

Seated around a large conference table in a room covered from wall to wall with images from a film that it was working on, a group of Pixar directors (referred to as the "brain trust") reviewed the work in progress. The director of the movie finished presenting the current version of the film, and listened to his colleagues as they gave comments and suggestions about how the movie could be improved. The discussion, which lasted for two hours, left the film director with a pool of suggestions and comments to consider.

Bringing a community of filmmakers together to help one another, these creative brain-trust sessions are common practice at Pixar and have resulted in the production of eleven highly successful feature films. Individuals working at all levels—from designers to directors—recognize the value of working in an environment where collaboration is not only encouraged by Pixar's leaders, but required.

When asked, the executives at Pixar repeatedly discounted the role that creative genius has played in making the company so successful. Instead, they give credit for their accomplishments to the role the entire team has played in encouraging a culture of collaboration throughout the company.[3] Facilitating interaction among employees at all levels, this culture of collaboration has led to the "all for one and one for all" mentality at Pixar—a mentality that, if adopted, would greatly benefit school districts engaged in Collaborative School Improvement.

Like the leaders at Pixar, district leaders in Evansville recognized the importance of encouraging shared ideas and innovations, and supporting one another at all levels. Prompted by Emily's vision of cross-school collaboration, Evansville teams were provided the opportunity to connect. Having spent time in the schools getting to know their strengths and struggles, Emily had insight into innovations within the district. When one team struggled with a task (such as creating a plan for looking at student work), Emily leveraged her perspective and role to put that team in contact with a successful team. Additionally, Emily was uniquely positioned to act as a liaison between the district teams and the outside experts, offering valuable information to the experts about the schools and leveraging them most effectively.

Early in the process, Emily worked with the outside experts to create a mechanism for cross-school sharing. She realized that successes—whether big or small— were occurring at every school in the district, and she wanted each school to deliver information and to benefit from peer feedback. Emily hoped that all schools would gain insight about their own practices—as the Cynthia Heights team had—simply by standing before their peers to share their ideas and innovations. Our experience shows that these innovation-sharing sessions are most fruitful when they allow teams to talk about both their most and least successful ideas. Bringing attention to what is working and what isn't allows teams to be thoughtful about what they are doing and provides opportunities for them to solve problems together.

Engaging teams in protocols such as the Inquiring Introductions Protocol (see exhibit 6.1 following this chapter) and the Tuning Protocol is one way to ensure that teams are delving into successes and problems in an efficient and effective way.[4] District leaders must teach school teams to be specific about the steps the teams take toward improving their schools, so that individuals can recognize the contributions that they are making. This idea is often countercultural in typical school districts. However, teams that consistently use protocols when discussing their work can effectively engage in conversations about what's working and what isn't. Through learning the standard format for these conversations at districtwide meetings, school-based teams will be better equipped to engage their colleagues in similar discussions about the work that is happening within the school.

Because of their vantage point, outside experts are well equipped to link schools in collaboration. For instance, STTs in Chandler designed a plan for observing classroom practice, and they turned to the outside expert for assistance. The experts, who were in the unique position of hearing from all of the schools in the cohort, quickly recognized that two of the principals were tackling the same issue: how to schedule observations so that all teachers could observe and be observed in one day.

Principal Susie Avey was excited to talk about her team's success in setting up a plan to observe practice in classrooms throughout her middle school. Susie and her team had come up with an innovative way to ensure that all teachers had the opportunity to observe in their colleagues' classrooms, and the team created a tight schedule for the observations. When Susie told the outside experts about it, she stated that many of her team's tools were adapted from prior experience with classroom observation: her team had saved hours in the planning process simply because it tapped into its resources and made use of already effective practices. In short, Susie and her team were not reinventing the wheel.

On a planning call with another principal from the cohort, the outside expert recognized how valuable Susie's tools might be to his team, which was working hard to come up with a schedule for observing practice. Putting the two school principals in contact with each other, the outside expert encouraged them to share their ideas and discuss the challenges that they were facing. On a follow-up call later in the month, the outside expert discovered that the second principal and his team had used Susie's plan as a starting point for creating their own schedule for observing practice. By leveraging his collaboration with Susie, the colleague principal not only saved time, but also produced a plan that would be useful to his school immediately.

Structuring Opportunities to Connect

While the value of sharing is clear, creating these opportunities requires a focused and intentional effort. Districts can structure opportunities for teams to share their innovations by using protocols or providing opportunities for casual conversations among teachers. Two keys: teams must be given adequate time to *collect* data from their colleagues and to *use* the information that they collect. A variety of venues within districts can be made available to transformation teams and schools for connection. Three venues are outlined in figure 6.1.

CELEBRATING SUCCESS

At the beginning of the school year in Evansville, school teams joined with their colleagues in celebrating all that they had accomplished since they started engaging in CSI. At Stringtown Elementary School, the song "Celebration" played in the background as food and prizes were spread throughout the school media center. In this setting, the transformation team reminded school administrators, teachers, and staff of the previous year's gains in student math proficiency. This beginning-of-year celebration reinvigorated everyone involved in the work, but it also marked where the school had started, where it was in the process, and where it hoped to go.

The value of celebrating success

As teachers left the celebration at Stringtown Elementary last fall, the halls were abuzz with comments such as "We did it!" and "For the first time in a long time, my kids feel like they're doing something well." Taking the time to acknowledge a school's success often gives much-needed inspiration to the students who are at the heart of the improvement process. Students and teachers appreciate the recognition of their effort. Within CSI, celebrating success involves more than just patting individuals on the back for their hard work. It also provides an opportunity for teams to acknowledge what is working and to internalize best practices.

Teams in Evansville regularly used protocols such as the Success Analysis Protocol (see exhibit 6.2 at the end of this chapter) to explore their successes in depth. For instance, at the start of a district training session, one principal recounted a personal success in leadership. He described his experience preparing for a staff meeting that was going to be led by one of the teachers and explained that, as part

FIGURE 6.1		
VENUES FOR SHARING		
Transformation team training sessions	*School-based sessions*	*Virtual connections*
▪ Occur at the district level ▪ Involve district and school trans-formation teams ▪ Provide opportunities for cross-school sharing	▪ Occur at the school level ▪ Utilize time during staff meetings ▪ Provide opportunities to share with school leaders and teachers	▪ Occur both across the district and within schools ▪ Provide alternative ways to connect and share

of the preparation, he asked the facilitating teacher to role-play with him. He asked her to present the whole meeting to him just as she was planning to present it to the staff. At first wary, the teacher later told him how helpful the process had been. She told him how much more prepared she felt to lead the session after they role-played, and she said she planned to use that method to prepare for other meetings, as well as for classroom teaching. As the principal shared this conversation with his peers, other school leaders realized that they could provide this same type of support for the teachers in their buildings.

Another team member described the success that her school experienced when the transformation team started its monthly meetings by reminding the staff members of where they had been and where they were going. This team member—who acknowledged that teachers were not feeling connected with the improvement process because of all of the day-to-day demands of their jobs—realized that taking the time to ensure that everyone was on the same page at the start of each meeting was integral to the success of the work. During the Success Analysis protocol, she shared her staff's positive response to starting sessions this way, and others teams decided to implement the same idea in their meetings.

Providing opportunities to celebrate successes

Any sincere celebration—regardless of where it takes place or how it looks—can have a positive impact on students, teachers, school leaders, the district, and the community. We offer as suggestions the following examples of celebrations in which we have been involved, and encourage each district to tailor its celebrations to meet the needs of schools, of the district, and of the community.

Perhaps the most frequent form of celebration that we see is embedded in the district training sessions. The value of celebrating during these sessions is that the individual school teams and the district team are both involved. In this type of gathering, teams are hearing about successes, internally documenting what is working at other schools, and making note of how certain approaches might look if they were tailored to meet their own school's specific needs. In addition, these opportunities provide the district team with valuable information about what schools are doing that is working, and offer insight into how teams are making the process their own.

Celebrations might occur at individual schools and involve people outside of the transformation team, including administrators, teachers, and students. In this scenario, the celebration is really about sharing rewards with the individuals who are most closely involved in the work—the teachers and students. The value of having a celebration at a school is that it builds excitement and reminds everyone involved of the importance of the improvement process.

When possible, opportunities to celebrate successes should reach beyond the district and into the community. Just as it "takes a village to raise a child," community support often plays an integral role for schools engaging in CSI. Outside of district- and school-based celebrations, districts may choose to celebrate their successes with the community. This type of celebration involves parents and other community members, inviting them to share in school improvement. Community celebrations may take place during PTA meetings or school open houses, or they may be part of a larger community event. These celebrations provide opportunities for administrators and teachers to go outside the school, garner support from individuals within the community, and publicly acknowledge the hard work that students and teachers are putting forth.

At the heart of these celebrations—regardless of what shape they take—should be recognizing improvements in teaching and increases in student learning. The work that schools engage in requires following a series of steps that will lead to long-term goals. Increases in student learning are unfortunately not immediate, but there will be other things to celebrate in the short run, such as building awareness of student work as data, consistently using effective meeting practices, progressing from one step in the process to the next, and building a community of learners. Leaders should be aware that all of these relatively small accomplishments are improving teaching and learning; therefore, they should encourage teams to celebrate these successes and provide opportunities for them to savor their accomplishments.

CONCLUSION

Amid the process of inquiry-based school improvement—identifying school-based priority needs and implementing solutions that address a root cause—schools and the district gain value from taking time to connect with each other about the work in which they are engaged. This often-neglected practice refines effective school improvement efforts as schools learn from one another's experiences. Simultaneously, districts become better informed about the schools' needs and successes. Isolation has characterized the profession of teaching and the field of education more generally—to their detriment—for too long.[5]

■

TAKEAWAYS

- *Celebrate good times: connecting for the purpose of sharing innovations and celebrating successes is an integral component of CSI.* Schools, their transformation teams, and the district each receive value when they connect with one another. Connecting unleashes the creativity and innovation that otherwise exists only in successful pockets. When school teams share strategies and strengths, they increase the capacity for widescale improvements in teaching and learning.
- *Just do it: while opportunities to connect take on a variety of shapes, the district's role is to ensure that they happen.* Leaders are positioned to facilitate cross-school collaboration, connecting teams that can benefit from one another's work. The district transformation team (and, most notably, the district lead) has the responsibility to make connecting a priority, and to design opportunities to share innovations and celebrate successes in a structured and productive way.
- *Embrace the good; learn from the bad: opportunities for connecting can be enhanced when the DTT closely follows the work of school teams, thus illuminating common challenges and best practices.* When a district understands the work in which schools are engaged, it is better equipped to build upon existing best practices and alleviate common challenges that schools encounter.

EXHIBIT 6.1

INQUIRING INTRODUCTIONS PROTOCOL

Inquiring Introductions was informed by research on effective Professional Learning Communities and other types of collaborative teams. In effective collaborative work, members ask each other questions—or inquire—about their practices, experiences, and beliefs. They develop deep and shared understandings of each other's practices through thoughtful and sustained questioning.

The purpose of Inquiring Introductions is twofold:

1. To learn about each other
2. To improve questioning skills

Steps

1. Create groups of 4–7 people.
2. Ask for one volunteer to go first. This person will be the first *introducer*. Other participants will be *colleagues* for this round.
3. The introducer states ONLY her name, subject taught, and grade level taught. For example: "My name is Anne Jones. I teach Earth Science in the 8th grade."
4. Colleagues ask questions to uncover more information about the introducer.

Notes

The guidelines below provide the structure of the protocol. If you don't follow the guidelines, you will not fulfill the purpose of the protocol.

- Colleagues can only ask questions that are related to the introducer's most immediate statement. For example, if the introducer says, "I am Anne Jones. I teach 8th grade Earth Science, "a colleague may ask, "How did you get interested in Earth Science?" This guideline is designed to help participants practice staying within the introducer's line of comment rather than going off on a tangent or connecting the introducer's sharing to something about themselves.
- Colleagues cannot ask a second question until all colleagues have asked their first question. This guideline is designed to help participants practice sharing air time and listening.

Modification

This protocol can be easily modified to help teams explore a variety of topics. All you need to do is change the introducer's opening statement in Step 3. For example, if a team wanted to explore their ideas about why students struggle to understand the concept of density, the introducer could open with their name and one idea about the root cause of the problem.

Source: Dr. Anne Jones

EXHIBIT 6.2

SUCCESS ANALYSIS PROTOCOL

The *analysis* of what makes a practice successful is the purpose of the protocol. The goal is *neither* to affirm that it was successful *nor* to brainstorm how to make it even more successful.

1. Reflect on an event or practice that your team could call a "success." (2 minutes)

2. Divide into groups of two or three (with different successes). (1 minute)

3. One team member describes their "success" and their specific behaviors (not the team's behaviors) that led to that success. Remember, the focus should not be on providing evidence that it was successful, but on what behaviors/routines/etc. helped it to succeed. This is not to be perceived as bragging—but to be an opportunity to be an analytical exercise about specific behaviors. (2–3 minutes uninterrupted)

> It is sometimes unclear what is being asked for and the overall facilitator can give some examples of "behaviors" that contribute to success (e.g., distribute agendas in advance with a list of things to bring . . . electronically distribute minutes . . . share feedback publicly . . . begin with willing people . . . acknowledge concerns but not let them prevent action).

4. If needed, the other members may ask **clarifying questions.*** Then all members work to define what made this practice successful and how it was different from other practices. Members should discuss specifically what the individual **did** and why was it successful. Participants may ask **probing questions**** and the presenter's participation is encouraged. Stay completely focused on one person for the entire 5 minutes. All participants should take notes of the specific behaviors that contributed to success. (2–3 minutes)

    REPEAT STEPS 3 and 4 FOR EACH MEMBER OF THE GROUP — 2 or 3 rounds

5. The whole group then takes 5 minutes to consider a list of the behaviors that led to the success.

6. A general discussion of the implication of the list follows.

***Clarifying questions** help the "asker" and should be those that provide facts and context (e.g., how many people, how often do you meet, how long were you on the job, etc.).

****Probing questions** are designed to help the other person think more deeply and reflectively about the issue and/or their role.

Source: Adapted from the National School Reform Faculty ("NSRF Materials," www.nsrfharmony.org/protocol/a_z.html)

CHAPTER 7

Leverage Expertise

Building Capacity to Sustain CSI

Driven by a desire to implement the inquiry cycle with fidelity, deepen the impact of the work, and make it sustainable, the Portland leadership team tapped into outside expertise: it hired an inquiry expert to lead training sessions and coach schools. The team does not regret the decision: district leaders have received continuous positive feedback from school leaders and teachers who appreciate having access to such expertise. However, PPS leaders worry about sustainability: would providing these resources drive long-lasting improvements in instruction? They know firsthand how having an outside perspective can be so valuable—especially for teachers and leaders who stand knee-deep in their improvement efforts. But they wonder how to use the outside expert to build internal capacity as well. After all, external experts are, by definition, external. They can't simply take up residence in the district: if they did, their influence would cease to carry as much weight. How could district leaders continue to leverage the outside experts without creating a reliance on them that would jeopardize the sustainability of the work after they left?

THE PROBLEM

Many districts seek external expertise. Having a pair of eyes that is objective and less focused on your internal experiences and stresses can be crucial to making informed decisions—especially throughout the details of the CSI practices. You may have confidence that all the CSI threads you're weaving will one day become a beautiful masterpiece, but for now, from your up-close perspective, they just look like a jumble of string. Someone who can stand back and see where you are in the process—who can provide direction about what steps should happen next and point out places where the work is developing flaws—can provide immense value. Without external expertise, you might give up on this challenging masterpiece you're weaving and return to your prior ways of doing business.

The added value of external expertise can increase the likelihood of success. There's a fine balance that you have to strike when calling on expertise, though, because leveraging an external provider tends to happen on a spectrum: if you pull too hard on the expert, you become dependent and cannot grow (think of expensive, drawn-out relationships with consultants). If you pull too little, the expert's insight has minimal influence and you could stagnate (the expert's light shines only for a fleeting moment and then goes out). Pulling just the right amount means that you fully understand and apply the expert's wisdom. It also means that you prepare up front for the expert's departure by training your own newly minted inside experts (DTT members) to take the reins after the expert leaves.

Although it's easy for districts to under- or overutilize outside expertise, learning to effectively leverage expertise is an essential practice of CSI. The problem we tackle in this chapter is how to effectively leverage the resource of outside expertise in a way that builds internal capacity to lead the work, not in a way that replaces or even diminishes the role of district leaders.

EFFECTIVELY LEVERAGING RESOURCES

Narrowing the focus (as explored in chapter 4) provides a context for districts and schools to intentionally direct their resources. With fewer initiatives receiving the focus of improvement efforts, districts can invest available financial resources into the areas of highest priority. However, to fully support the districtwide implementation of inquiry as a sustainable process, districts need to invest as well in building the capacity of their individuals. This chapter explores how a district can leverage outside expertise to build internal capacity for the work of inquiry-based school improvement.

Sustainability is key in leveraging external expertise: many improvement efforts focus on the initial introduction of new methods and instructional strategies. Teachers and school leaders commonly attend professional conferences and learn useful strategies, but return to the school environment with little follow-up on the implementation of new practices or on their collaboration with colleagues. This pattern is problematic, because meaningful changes to instruction require ongoing attention—including time and opportunities for collaboration and reflection—if they are to impact classroom instruction. When districts fail to dedicate their resources to ensuring ongoing and relevant support, they are unlikely to see lasting changes in teaching and learning.

As researcher Mary M. Kennedy noted: in teaching, "both God and the devil are in the details."[1] Districts can make a difference by leveraging resources to support the capacity for implementation: with enough time, teachers can cultivate a deep understanding of how to embed new strategies, resources, and tools in their instructional practice. With sufficient guidance from internal and external sources, teachers can refine their instructional practice to support real gains in student achievement.

BUILDING INTERNAL CAPACITY

Implementing an inquiry-based cycle as part of CSI requires dramatic shifts in the ways districts and schools do improvement. Making any change can be challenging, especially when it involves cultural and behavioral shifts. However, having support through a change—having someone who can build you up and encourage your efforts, shouldering some of the burden until you're strong enough to carry it alone—can increase the duration and success of the new behavior. As schools and districts naturally encounter confusion while implementing the shifts in practices required by Collaborative School Improvement, they can benefit from the expertise and perspective of an outside expert. In varied capacities, we at Education Direction support districts in implementing CSI. From our experience working as outside experts, we understand the specific needs that emerge when districts and schools engage in new practices through inquiry-based school improvement. We bring this perspective to this chapter: we understand the potential contributions an outside expert can make, and the ways districts can best capitalize on this value. We also understand the things that don't work well, and we'll discuss those, too.

To clearly distinguish between our role as narrators and our role as outside experts for the districts mentioned in this book, we refer to our outside expert work in this chapter specifically in the third person. Our hope is that this approach will illuminate the many functions of an outside expert, and the ways districts can leverage expertise—both inside and outside the district—to better support sustainable, inquiry-based school improvement efforts.

We also intentionally refer to *outside experts* in the plural form. This reflects our belief that an organization, which pulls from a wider breadth of experience working across districts and has a more varied set of instructional and school leadership expertise in its ranks, offers greater value to a district than an individual. We have also found that as a group of individuals, an organization is not as prone to the influences of life changes (career, family, etc.) that can quickly and detrimentally remove an individual expert from a district.

The overarching and long-term objective of engaging outside providers in the work of CSI is singular: to build the capacity for inquiry-based school improvement across a district. One of the outside providers' most important jobs is to foster an ongoing partnership between schools and the district. When the experts' work with the district is finished, all future improvement efforts rest in the hands of this partnership, so the experts must invest in making it strong.

It is helpful from the outset, then, to plan for the outside providers' departure. Keeping this endpoint in mind will encourage districts to build sufficient internal capacity to shoulder the work after the outside providers' participation has concluded. With this long-term vision in mind, districts are better positioned to identify and focus on the skills that they will need to independently ensure sustainability of the work. Likewise, districts are more apt to leverage the expertise of the outside providers in areas that build capacity—ensuring a long-term implementation of CSI—when they're aware that the outside experts' presence is temporary.

Whether a district has the resources to engage outside providers, its focus should remain the same: to build an ongoing partnership with schools that supports long-term, inquiry-based Collaborative School Improvement, and to leverage its resources to develop internal leadership capacity.

Role of Outside Experts

In the spring of 2010, Gina Vukovich began searching for an outside provider to help implement the Data Wise Improvement Process, the inquiry cycle that the district had adopted.[2] As the district lead in Chandler, Gina believed that an outside expert would help her district transformation team most effectively support schools in implementing the process.

Because implementing a data-driven inquiry cycle requires new skills and rescripts standard leadership roles within the district and individual schools, the district may elect to bring in outside experts who can support the process. While district personnel like Gina have some familiarity with the identified inquiry cycle, it is likely that they lack extensive experience in its implementation—especially across many schools at once. In support of district efforts, outside experts bring perspective and accountability that the district may struggle to provide early in the implementation of the inquiry cycle. Employing providers with experience and perspective to lead schools in the cycle during the early years will minimize hassles and confusion; having help from someone who's done it before can make all the difference. Additionally, with trained outside experts holding the reins at the outset, district leaders can devote time to engaging with the DTT and gaining a solid understanding of how to lead this work into the future.

Outside experts can offer direct professional development to school teams on the steps of the inquiry cycle, as well as on the soft skills that support its effective implementation (a topic discussed at greater length in chapter 3). However, experts may also extend support in other areas relevant to the work. Districts can decide how to engage with and leverage the outside providers, tailoring that interaction to reflect their unique context and needs (see table 7.1).

Value of Outside Experts

Let's get a better sense for what Gina was hoping to gain by engaging an outside expert. She wasn't looking to shift responsibility elsewhere: she was competent in her current role and committed to implementing the inquiry-based improvement process in her district. However, she knew that she and her team would benefit from having experienced mentors. To this end, she sought an expert that would meet the needs of her district. She'd seen outside providers lend essential expertise to the work of CSI in a variety of districts. Particularly in the early stages of implementation, outside providers support districts in launching an inquiry cycle that improves teaching at the classroom level, and they simultaneously work to build sustainable leadership capacity across the district. Gina knew that an outside expert would bring valuable perspective and accountability to her district.

Perspective

Targeting specific areas, outside experts bring unique perspective and focus to the CSI work. Through their experience working with districts diverse in size, demographics, and leadership structure, outside experts have gained a comprehensive view of the work; their perspective allows them to see how each school can effectively structure the work of inquiry-based improvement.

Because of their experience, outside experts are able to anticipate stumbling blocks or sticking points, particularly in the way inquiry informs instructional practice. When a district or school encounters a challenge, the outside provider can share information about how other districts have negotiated similar hurdles.

TABLE 7.1

POTENTIAL ROLES OF AN OUTSIDE PROVIDER WITHIN CSI

Potential roles of outside providers within CSI	Examples from case study districts
Support the district in the development of a strategic plan	Questioned by a board member about the sustainability of Data Wise implementation in the Chandler Unified School District, the district realized the need to create a plan to support the long-term implementation of the process. With this need identified, the district approached the outside providers for assistance in creating a five-year strategic plan, outlining specific objectives and the steps to ensure a focus on each. The outside providers used their expertise with other districts implementing similar objectives to support the district in crafting a plan that clarified a path for sustainability in the work of inquiry-based school improvement.
Support the district in the development or refinement of a school improvement plan	District leaders in Portland, Oregon, identified a lack of alignment between inquiry-driven school improvement efforts and the existing school improvement plan (SIP) the district required schools to submit. Seeing an opportunity to create alignment by making the SIP template more relevant, district leaders worked with the outside providers to create a revised SIP template that more closely aligned with the inquiry cycle in which schools were engaged. The resulting SIP more closely mirrored the work of the schools (using similar terms and providing places to fill in goals and expectations) and met compliance requirements for the plan set by the state for all Title 1 schools.
Build the district's capacity to lead schools in the identified inquiry cycle	Acknowledging the need to deeply understand the inquiry cycle they expected schools to implement, members of the district transformation team in Chandler attended each Data Wise training session for district schools. Following each session, the DTT met individually with the outside providers to discuss how it could best support the steps of the work presented within the training, focusing particularly on providing schools with high-quality feedback.
Train schools in the implementation of the identified inquiry cycle	The Evansville Vanderburgh School Corporation hired outside providers to lead all its schools through the Data Wise Improvement Process. This support involved four onsite training sessions through the school year in years one and two, supplemented by webinars to support school leaders and coaches. These training sessions not only focused on the steps of the Data Wise process, but also provided opportunities for engagement in protocols and reflection on the implementation of the work within the school setting.
Address specific school needs	In their second year of implementation of the Data Wise Improvement Process, schools in Evansville found themselves facing increasingly different challenges. To address this issue, the outside providers allocated time for school-specific coaching, providing an opportunity for individual teams to bring questions or challenges to discussion. The outside providers' experiences working across districts and abilities to speak to these challenges helped schools solve problems and maintain the work's momentum.

This wealth of applied learning is a chief asset that an outside provider can leverage on behalf of the district.

An external perspective can also add value to an environment experiencing change. Anyone who has worked in a school or district setting understands the complex cultures and relationships that develop within and across these institutions. As educators, we have emotional investments in our work and in the students we serve. Therefore, when we encounter change, we experience emotion associated with the implications of that change. This is precisely where outside experts can offer valuable assistance. Removed from the immediate details of the unique culture in a district, outside experts are better positioned to see the forest through the trees. Their perspective is unmarred by existing investments in programs, processes, or roles.

Accountability

While *accountability* has earned a narrow connotation amidst the era of No Child Left Behind, we propose a broader application. The concept has tremendous value when it is used to ensure effective implementation of school improvement efforts. Accountability within CSI involves ensuring that the work is focused on the instructional core, and ultimately, that implemented changes will directly impact student learning. Particularly in the early stages of the work—when individuals may become preoccupied with the details of the inquiry process itself—outside experts can ensure that schools not only complete each step of the inquiry cycle, but that they also maintain a focus on the work of inquiry as a vehicle for driving improvements in teaching. Keeping schools on track to their destination even amid process-induced turbulence is a significant example of how outside providers add value.

Frequently, districts and outside providers share in the work of setting standards for accountability. Shared engagement in this piece of CSI supports building internal capacity, as the outside experts are able to provide insight into areas of particular importance while the district ensures completion of high-quality work.

In Chandler, the district leveraged the expertise of the outside providers in ensuring accountability throughout the first year of CSI by asking teams to submit specific evidence of their work following each training session. This requirement ensured that teams maintained fidelity to the inquiry cycle, and provided an opportunity for them to receive thoughtful and informative feedback on their work. The outside providers offered feedback that supported Chandler school transformation teams in effectively identifying a narrow, focused need and associated root cause, and in monitoring progress throughout the year. The outside providers also gave specific suggestions to focus attention on the details of data collection, particularly in relation to progress monitoring (see table 7.2). By collecting reports and offering responsive feedback, the outside experts supported the accountability efforts in the district as well as the work of the school teams.

Leveraging the expertise of the outside providers in Chandler not only informed the work of each school, but also supported capacity building at the district. In this process, the outside experts shared the feedback they provided to schools with the district lead, thereby developing her understanding of the most important elements in each step of the work. The outside experts cleared the path and offered a successful example for the DTT, which would take over much of the work in coming years. Thus, in the second year of CSI, the DTT in Chandler adopted the role of providing feedback to school teams, consulting the outside providers about questions it encountered in the process. This transfer of responsibility enhanced the DTT's understanding of the inquiry cycle and empowered it to hold schools accountable for effectively implementing the work into the future. By providing feedback to school teams, the DTT developed a deeper understanding of each school's progress in the cycle and discovered areas where schools would benefit from additional support. This process also provided an important ideological shift for schools, as they began looking to the district—rather than to the outside provider—for support in the work.

Traditional conceptions of accountability can hinder districts from fully leveraging the expertise of the outside providers. For instance, having outside experts simply "check off" the work fails in three key areas: leveraging expertise, supporting the work of teams, and building capacity within the district. As noted in the preceding example in Chandler, developing a broader understanding of accountability supports the ongoing effectiveness of the work. Yet, realizing the benefits of accountability requires a deep understanding of the inquiry process itself—knowledge that the outside experts can foster within the district. In this manner, outside providers' expertise and perspective can cultivate the district's ability to offer meaningful feedback to and encourage accountability among school teams.

Engaging the Outside Expert to Maximize Value

While the outside providers can bring valuable perspective and focus—as we have seen in the examples from Chandler—the DTT bears the responsibility of fully

TABLE 7.2

OUTSIDE PROVIDER FEEDBACK TO CHANDLER HIGH SCHOOL

	Chandler High School: *Plan to Assess Progress (PtAP) Feedback*
Overall comments	■ Your PtAP includes information about each of the data collection points (short-, medium-, and long-term). ■ Clear distinction and identification of the roles of teachers, departments, and the team in data reporting.
Short-term	■ Will teachers meet by department to discuss this data and how it can be used to inform instruction? ■ What process or protocol will teachers use to analyze this data?
Medium-term	■ Did you collect any data prior to the implementation of the instructional strategy that you could input here as a baseline? If so, this will give you a better idea of improvement after the implementation of the strategy. ■ Will your sample of students being assessed be random? ■ It's great to see that you have a plan for sharing the data with the whole school (at monthly faculty meetings). You may want to consider creating a chart to graph student progress and making it visible for all teachers to see. ■ For your goal, decide on an ambitious and achievable percentage. For more information on this, refer to the *Data Wise* book, pages 149–153.
Long-term	■ Enter last year's AIMS scores in the baseline column so you can refer to them easily. ■ Do you anticipate seeing greater growth in specific strands? If so, you may consider accounting for this in the goals that you set. ■ Are your goals for the percentage of students who are proficient? Again, enter in an actual value for the percentage of growth that you hope to see.

Source: Education Direction

actualizing this potential value. Meeting this goal requires the DTT to have a deep understanding of schools and their needs. While outside providers will develop an awareness of schools' needs, the district team's localized understanding of schools can provide a more comprehensive picture. With such understanding, the DTT is better equipped to leverage the expertise in a manner that supports the schools' specific needs.

At the end of the second year of CSI in Evansville, the DTT sat around a conference table discussing the unique challenges that each school team was experiencing—challenges that were as varied as the schools themselves. From the DTT's perspective, it seemed that as the schools took greater ownership for the work, their challenges multiplied. In response, the district leveraged the outside expert to allocate specific time to meet with individual school teams and discuss their unique hurdles. The DTT observed these coaching sessions, which served to build their capacity to fill this role in coming years. The outside experts' individual support of schools showed these schools that the district was responding specifically to their needs, which reinforced the effective district-school partnership.

Effectively leveraging the expertise of outside providers requires the DTT to have a clear, long-term vision for CSI. This vision will drive the duration and manner in which the team engages the outside providers. Additionally, it will guide intentional decision making and support the achievement of long-term objectives. The DTT may decide to engage the outside experts in developing this vision and clearly defining its goals. In Chandler, district leaders developed a five-year strategic plan with the direct support of the outside experts. Detailed in scope, this strategic plan framed three program goals that clarified the district's objectives and informed the role of the outside experts (see box 7.1).

HOW TO CHOOSE AN OUTSIDE PROVIDER

Arm in arm with district leaders, outside providers both lead and support—clearing the path and showing the way as needed—thereby enabling the leaders to confidently take the reins of their newly powerful, inquiry-based school improvement. Outside experts support capacity building across the district within the work of inquiry-based school improvement. CSI is valuable only as much as it informs instructional practice, and outside experts have the knowledge for successfully implementing an inquiry cycle, which will drive meaningful changes in instruction and ultimately improve student learning.

BOX 7.1

EXCERPT FROM CUSD FIVE-YEAR STRATEGIC PLAN

Target end state

Ultimate specific program goals

1. The ultimate goal of the program is to increase student learning by aiding participating schools in developing collaborative cultures of data-informed decision making, focusing intently on classroom instruction as the greatest lever for school improvement.

2. For the schools in CUSD, this means that the district will provide one year of intensive Data Wise training followed by one year of support to ensure that school teams are continuing to implement the process with fidelity. The goal is to involve all schools in the district in this program over a five-year period.

3. In addition to building capacity at the school level, CUSD will engage a group of leaders, the district transformation team, which will be responsible for learning the process, providing feedback and support to schools, and holding schools responsible for implementing the process with fidelity both during and long after the five-year program.

Requirements

Role of the district transformation team

Support of participating schools:

1. Year one: ten full-day sessions with Education Direction, ongoing support, and feedback from district transformation team.

2. Year two: four full-day sessions with Education Direction, ongoing support, and feedback from district transformation team.

3. Year three: submission of newly conceived school improvement plan to district transformation team for review and feedback.

4. All years: schools must provide evidence of having implemented the Data Wise process (as documented by the new school improvement plan).

Source: Chandler Unified School District, Chandler, Arizona

After a district has decided to bring in outside expertise, it faces another big decision: how to locate the right provider. To inform a district's selection, the following section identifies nine essential characteristics of effective outside providers. Though the list is not exhaustive, each element affects a provider's capacity to make effective contributions to the work of CSI. Outside providers who have these qualities (see box 7.2) will enhance the district's ability to drive meaningful instructional shifts and build the necessary capacity to maintain those improvements.

Are Former Teachers and Administrators

Anyone who has spent time teaching in the classroom understands that this experience provides insight unavailable elsewhere. Where else could you develop strategies for handling flying sandwiches or feuding teenagers? Where else could you discover how to give a lesson that keeps students' eyes from glazing over and actually leads to measurable improvement? Outside experts who have spent time in the classroom are aware of the unique challenges of the profession, and they have insight into how children learn. This understanding will enable experts to guide school improvement efforts that focus on instructional change. Therefore, classroom teaching experience is essential to being an effective outside expert.

BOX 7.2

QUALITIES OF AN EFFECTIVE OUTSIDE PROVIDER TO SUPPORT CSI

Effective outside providers:

- Are former teachers and administrators
- Maintain a focus on the instructional core
- Understand of how to align work within the local context
- Demonstrate experience in forming a partnership with a district
- Are learners at heart
- Have an exit strategy
- Present in a clear and engaging manner
- Use the practices they teach
- Demonstrate evidence of increased student learning

School experience—whether in the role of teacher or administrator—provides a lens for understanding the challenges that arise throughout the improvement cycle. Providers with this perspective have experienced common hurdles, like ill-spent faculty meeting time and resistance to change, and can strategically avoid those pitfalls in the process of implementing CSI.

In addition to developing street smarts, providers who have survived the jungle earn credibility with the other explorers. In other words, teachers and school leaders value the perspective of outside experts who have understanding of the profession grounded in classroom and leadership experience. Shared experience fosters trust, and when schools trust their expert guides, they are willing to make tough changes. When experts understand firsthand the effort it takes to refocus the energy of thirty fifth-graders after recess and the frustration of having to implement changing initiatives each year, they can speak to teachers as colleagues. Understanding the challenges—and joys—of the profession situates the outside providers to build rapport with individuals throughout the district.

Maintain a Focus on the Instructional Core

Research demonstrates that high-quality instruction is the single most important factor in increasing student achievement. While conversations on school improvement naturally include topics outside the realm of instruction, effective outside experts maintain a focus on the instructional core. They know that improving classroom instruction is the most powerful lever for increasing student learning, so they concentrate on creating changes in instructional practice.

Some non-CSI school improvement efforts suggest making changes to the structures of schools—scheduling, afterschool programs, etc.—instead of to the core of instructional practice. Outside experts who primarily emphasize such changes in structure miss the mark; effective ones focus continually on the interaction of the teacher, students, and classroom content, and allow relevant structural changes to follow.

Outside providers who focus on the instructional core ensure that the inquiry cycle becomes the vehicle for transforming teaching and learning, and do not overemphasize doing the inquiry cycle "right." These providers chart a course toward improving teaching and learning, and use the inquiry cycle as the means to get there, not as the end goal. The inquiry cycle is valuable only if it informs and improves instruction—the vision of CSI. Providers who focus on developing skills but neglect the outcome are akin to a dieter who, hoping to improve his overall health through weight loss, eats only rice. While it is likely that he will shed pounds, he has neglected the larger objective of improving his health in the process. Skilled outside experts, then, use an inquiry cycle as a tool for schools to understand their needs and implement instructional changes to drive meaningful improvements.

Understand How to Align Work Within the Local Context

"One size fits all" may work for cheap hats, but it has no place in education. That's why prepackaged improvement programs regularly fail to align with the unique existing structures and language within each district and state context. How could they align? They're meant to fit any district, but, with that intent, they actually fit no district. Effective outside experts understand this: they are equipped to apply broad improvement principles to specific situations. Building on the existing culture of the district without losing the essential principles of inquiry-based school improvement, outside providers offer flexibility by responding to the specific needs of a district and its schools.

For instance, districts engaging in CSI are likely to notice that the required state and/or district improvement plans contain language that differs in terminology (although not meaning) from the district's identified inquiry cycle. This is where the outside providers can make a big difference: through exploring the existing state template, the providers can help align the state's language with the district's inquiry cycle. Such alignment is significant: it prevents the introduction of new language that would burden schools already facing a multitude of changes.

Knowing how to align the big-picture work within a local context is an important part of an experienced outside expert's skill set. Effective experts have the capacity to share how this process has looked in other districts and which ideas might support alignment—with your help—in your own district.

Demonstrate Experience in Forming a Partnership with a District

Outside experts are perhaps most commonly typified as professional developers—individuals who enter a district or school primarily to present in front of teachers and principals. While this is one important task that effective outside experts perform through CSI, it is merely a fragment of the support that they offer through the implementation of inquiry-based school improvement. As with any systemic change that demands shifts in culture and procedure, CSI requires an ongoing investment of time and attention as new practices take hold over several years. As districts experience the nuances of implementing inquiry-based school improvement, they will benefit from support that goes beyond traditional training sessions and specifically drives capacity building and sustainability.

Therefore, districts should seek external providers who will maintain an ongoing partnership with the district to support these objectives. From this perspective, outside providers are positioned to develop an understanding of the existing experience and expertise of those within the district. The providers can then leverage this existing expertise to support areas of need, filling in the gaps where necessary. Effective outside experts view the district as a thought-partner in the work, rather than as a recipient of external know-how. Such a relationship supports the practice of leveraging expertise—both inside and outside the district.

Are Learners at Heart

Inquiry-based school improvement and data-based decision making are more complex than standard fix-its. They depend on and respond to the specific context in which they are implemented; while the inquiry process itself may be uniform across a district, the outcomes of the process will be school-specific.

With this in mind, effective outside experts empower schools with a means to address their needs, rather than simply handing them solutions. This reverses the relationship that can exist between outside providers as "experts" and school and district faculty as "recipients of knowledge." Within Collaborative School Improvement, capable outside providers partner with the district and schools, learning alongside them. Effective providers approach their role with this objective in mind, understanding that learning alongside the district leaders builds their own capacity and effectiveness within the district.

Have an Exit Strategy

As illustrated throughout this chapter, the long-term objective of having an outside expert's support is for the district to build capacity to lead the work across schools. Over time, this objective informs the ongoing interactions between the outside expert and district. From the beginning, however, it requires the expert to make a plan for exiting the district. While the exit strategy will likely evolve over time in response to the work in the district, such a plan will motivate an effective outside provider's forethought and priority for capacity building.

From the beginning of CSI implementation, district leaders in Evansville worked steadily to build the capacity of their internal resources, and they leveraged the outside provider to support their vision. As its internal capacity to lead grew, the district gradually reduced the number of on-site visits from the outside expert, and transferred responsibility from the outside expert to district coaches (again lever-aging an internal resource). To support their growth, the district leaders provided four training sessions co-led by the outside expert and coaches. Throughout their partnership, the outside provider cleared the path for district leaders, helping them implement changes and resolve challenges, thereby enabling them to take the reins as soon as they were ready.

Present in a Clear and Engaging Manner

"When's this guy going to finish talking? Isn't it about time to break for lunch? I don't have any idea how to apply what he's saying to my daily work." We have all sat uncomfortably at a conference or other professional development session as a presenter drones on about content that lacks a direct connection to our everyday work as educators. Without opportunities to explore this knowledge in the context of our lesson planning, instruction, or school leadership, we are unable to apply the content, and the lesson slips away amid our other responsibilities. In contrast, an effective outside provider creates context for teachers and school leaders to engage meaningfully with the skills they're learning. They can then effectively implement inquiry-based school improvement practices within each school in the district.

Holding training sessions is one way of engaging school transformation teams in the work of inquiry-based improvement: these sessions teach STTs to dig deeply into data, identify needs and corresponding root causes, and make instructional adjustments. Because the CSI process requires schools and districts to grasp some complex and urgent information, choosing an outside expert who can present well is a smart idea.

Good presenters make the content clear. They're engaging and interesting to listen to. Their presentations ensure that school teams develop a deep understand-ing of the inquiry cycle early on, which will set them up for success as they identify and implement instructional changes. By allowing STTs to engage in the work in a structured environment before they are responsible for sharing it with their faculty, good presenters provide authentic opportunities for linking theory with practice.

In Chandler, the outside expert framed training sessions around case studies. Within each training session, STTs engaged in the work collectively. They shared a common data set to develop an initial understanding and then applied the new skills and tools to their own environments and data. This expert's method—which balanced instructional time with opportunities to engage in the work—equipped the teams to anticipate stumbling blocks and reflect on school-specific implementation. Teams were then well positioned to bring the tools back to their schools.

Use the Practices They Teach

Inquiry-based school improvement is grounded in data-driven decision making. Effective outside providers should ground their work in the same techniques: collecting, analyzing, and utilizing data to inform practice. Districts should look for evidence that outside providers engage in the same practices that they expect of schools. Not only does this demonstrate a strong understanding of and capacity for using data, but it also ensures that the outside experts' services will respond directly to the needs of the schools and districts with which they work.

Collecting both quantitative and qualitative data enables the outside expert to ground professional development sessions in real content. This data also documents how the implementation of inquiry-based school improvement has affected the culture of individual schools and the district. An effective outside expert uses this data to monitor progress and demonstrates the practices that educators should be implementing: collaborating with colleagues, using data to inform instruction, and reviewing multiple sources of data to understand student thinking.

In Evansville, the outside expert regularly collected data from STTs at training sessions and surveyed the whole faculty at each school. Useful for both the provider and the district, this data became a tool for identifying areas for increased focus and growth. Because student achievement growth is the long-term objective of CSI, teachers have to shift the way they work together to discuss and utilize data. Measuring these changes demonstrated the effect of the outside expert and helped the district monitor progress. The collected data provided insight to individual school teams, and, when examined holistically districtwide, informed the outside expert's support. Figure 7.1 provides an example of the data school teams received.

Demonstrate Evidence of Increased Student Learning

Just as they practice what they preach by collecting various types of data, effective outside experts should demonstrate the effects of their work, most notably through improved student achievement. While shifts in practices among teachers and school leaders are evidence of the implementation of an inquiry cycle, these shifts are valuable only if they result in improvements in student learning. Districts hiring an outside expert should require evidence of student achievement growth in prior consulting work.

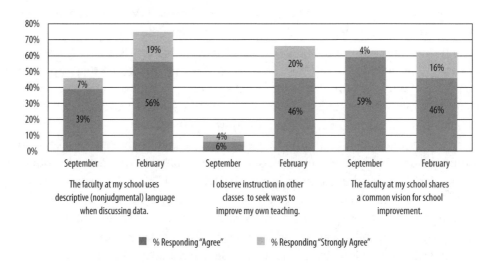

FIGURE 7.1

NORTH HIGH SCHOOL FACULTY SURVEY DATA

September 2010 to February 2011

■ % Responding "Agree"   ▨ % Responding "Strongly Agree"

LEVERAGING EXPERTISE WITH LIMITED FINANCIAL RESOURCES

Our experiences as outside experts have given us a deep understanding of how outside providers can add value to the work of CSI, and of how districts can best leverage providers to build their capacity to lead and engage in the work. From our experiences as teachers and administrators, we also understand that districts have many needs competing for finite financial resources, which can present a challenge to hiring an outside provider. This is particularly true in smaller districts, where professional development funds do not provide for an economy of scale available in larger districts.

When a district is able to engage an outside expert in simultaneous efforts among schools, it often finds that the return on investment is quite large. In one district with which we worked, the investment was less than $5,000 per school for a year of support in the implementation of the inquiry cycle. Given that this district also saw consistent growth in student learning over the two-year period in which it engaged in CSI (to date), the investment returned real dividends.

Even when financial limitations prohibit a district from engaging outside experts, districts can creatively leverage expertise both inside and outside their organization. Any district can benefit from cultivating what outside experts provide: perspective and accountability.

To gain additional perspective, leaders can reach out to other districts that have engaged in CSI. Generally, districts experienced in this work are proud of their accomplishments—shifts in practice and growth in student achievement—and are eager to share their learning with others. These experienced districts are also adept at identifying challenges they encountered and can provide valuable perspective in anticipating and overcoming these obstacles. Districts and schools may also gain perspective from a book study—particularly one that includes concrete examples of school improvement at the ground level. As evidenced by what Chandler did with *Data Wise* (see chapter 9), book studies can provide the context for collaboratively exploring the work of inquiry-based school improvement.

While outside experts can provide crucial accountability early in the implementation of an inquiry cycle, district personnel can soon prepare to fulfill this role, or fulfill it from the outset if outside expertise is not sought. The district lead or DTT collectively may review the work of schools, providing thoughtful feedback that supports high-quality work. Here again, seeking the perspective of districts that have engaged in this work can provide insight into how they adopted these responsibilities in a manner that supported the implementation of first-rate work across schools.

A WORD OF CAUTION

The district may hire an outside provider for expertise in the implementation of the inquiry cycle, only to develop a reliance on that person as the extra eyes, ears, and hands of the district. This is particularly understandable in the climate of typical districts, where individuals face myriad responsibilities that consume the valuable resource of time. While the outside expert can initially alleviate the mounting CSI tasks of those within the district, the addition of the outside provider should not decrease the district's total investment of time. In places where the outside expert is fulfilling roles the district will later adopt, the district can benefit from leveraging available time to build capacity. Districts that neglect capacity building will inhibit the long-term sustainability and effectiveness of their work. Viewing the outside expert only as an extra resource with whom to distribute work hinders the developing partnership between schools and the district within CSI.

CONCLUSION

In an era of decreasing resources in education, districts must effectively leverage their available resources, both internal (through calling on in-district experts) and external (through engaging outside experts). A district must create a clear vision for sustainable school improvement and identify steps for putting the vision into practice. An effective outside provider can offer crucial support in the early stages of implementation and will enable district leaders to carry the work forward. With such clarity and a focus on building internal capacity, the district can make informed decisions about where to invest and how to leverage resources. Internal and external resources should contribute to the implementation and sustainability of CSI efforts that return measurable improvements in teaching and student learning.

■

TAKEAWAYS

- *From training wheels to sustainability: the ultimate objective of leveraging an outside expert is to build district and school capacity to sustain the work of inquiry-based school improvement.* Frequently, districts engage an outside expert to support implementation of an inquiry cycle and guide school improvement efforts. While this can provide great value, the outside expert's ultimate objective is to build capacity within the district to maintain the work of inquiry-based school improvement. Outside experts partner with districts in order to build upon existing skills within the district. Successful districts will leverage expertise both inside the district (via coaches and teachers) and outside the district (via the knowledge and experience of outside providers).
- *Experts with a dream-team résumé: if districts decide to engage an outside expert, they should search for one with the following nine characteristics.* To be effective, outside experts should have spent time in the classroom (be former teachers and administrators), maintain a focus on the instructional core, understand how to align the work within a local context, demonstrate experience in forming a partnership with a district, be learners at heart,

have an exit strategy, present in a clear and engaging manner, use the practices they teach, and demonstrate evidence of increased student learning.

- *A partnership, not a stopgap: effectively leveraging the value of an outside expert requires time and deliberate attention.* While districts may be tempted to hire an outside provider to cover their lack of expertise or time, this choice can be detrimental to long-term school improvement efforts. Districts should use outside experts not as time-savers, but as a partners who can build the capacity of the district to lead the work. When districts invest time and attention into a partnership with an outside expert and learn to carry the work forward after the provider's departure, they will build sustainable school improvement efforts.

CHAPTER 8

Reflect and Refine

Making Regular Revisions for Continuous Improvement

After wrapping up its second year in the Data Wise Improvement Process, the district transformation team in Evansville was trying to figure out where it had missed the mark with some of its schools: the evidence showed minimal improvements in instructional strategies at a few schools. Tracing its process over months, the DTT identified a common shortcoming in the implementation of inquiry during the first year of work for these schools. The DTT noted that even the struggling schools had gone through the early steps of the inquiry cycle with flying colors and successfully identified a priority need. However, the problem lay in the solution: these schools had developed methods for addressing their respective needs that emphasized improving learning strategies for students, rather than improving teaching strategies. Bingo. No wonder that, after a full year of implementation, the district observed schools repeatedly struggling to generate meaningful instructional improvements—school teams were still focusing on student learning strategies rather than on instructional strategies. Seeing the problem empowered the DTT to refine its tactics for the coming year. One team member reflected, "As a DTT, we failed to provide enough direction to school teams to ensure that their work resulted in improvements to teaching practice. Some did it intuitively, or because they read the book chapters more carefully, but others needed more help from us. I wish we'd seen this earlier so we could have altered our strategy for this year, but I'm glad we have a structure for refining our practice over time so we won't be fixing this same problem next year."

THE PROBLEM

Just as inquiry lies at the heart of Collaborative School Improvement—serving as the means for identifying needs and then acting upon them—the practice of engaging in timely reflection is key to understanding results. Reflection highlights the connections between cause and effect, clarifying why events unfolded as they did. This clarity has dramatic implications for future work: when leaders thoughtfully consider how well their efforts realized their vision, they have the power to make relevant changes.

At both the school and district levels, teams that are dedicated to implementing the practices of CSI with fidelity often discount the importance of taking the time to reflect on the work that they are doing throughout the process. With the flurry of meetings, observations, and collaboration, teams have a lot on their plates. When they focus solely on implementing inquiry without reflecting on the day-to-day, push-and-pull results of their practice, they are unable to make essential refinements that will impact their current experience and inform their future planning. Wearing blinders is ironic in a data-saturated improvement method: if teams are willing to use data to inform their improvement work, shouldn't they take time to look at their own work as data for informing future practice?

By design, CSI serves as a framework for districts, guiding them through their improvement efforts. It is not intended to—and, indeed, cannot—function as a "plug and play" method. District leaders who successfully implement CSI practices are dedicated to thoughtfully refining their efforts, tailoring their work to their own schools. When leaders neglect the practices of reflecting and refining, CSI efforts will stagnate.

REFLECTING AND REFINING

As you know by this point in the book, CSI calls for districts to implement eight practices as they help schools improve—and reflecting and refining is the culminating practice. The art of being reflective is important to practitioners in the classroom setting who are continually refining what works with their students and what does not. It is equally important in CSI. There really is something to calling reflection an art: it's not a finite action that you can script and demand. Sure, there are tips and tactics, which we'll discuss throughout this chapter, but the *art* of reflection is something leaders can cultivate over time. It's a way of seeing—a lens that filters out unimportant details and highlights things that really make a difference (for better or for worse!) throughout the timeframe in question. When leaders sit back for a minute, prop up their feet, and talk with one another about where they've been—unleashing their minds to sift through the preceding hours, days, or months—they discover crucial details they might have otherwise passed over. Like panning for gold, being reflective takes time and commitment. It requires a willingness to discern valuable flakes amid mountains of minutiae. Being reflective also calls on leaders to sit up, slide their feet back to the floor, and mobilize their teams to make crucial changes. Reflection fosters understanding, which empowers leaders to make spot-on refinements.

As leaders in school improvement efforts, districts have the responsibility to be reflective about their practices. Reflection is not a one-time event; it requires a constant willingness to consider how the work could be improved and a determination to document and then implement those enhancements.

By taking the time to analyze what you have already done for the purpose of informing your future work, CSI will become more "your own" and less of a program that you have adopted. You'll find that you can improve your experience with each CSI practice—from adopting an inquiry cycle to leveraging the expertise of an outside provider—when you actively engage in reflection and refinement. In the opening vignette to this chapter, we saw the DTT reflect on its work and then plan to refine the support it offered to schools in the coming year. Through reflection, this DTT discovered that it needed to support schools in making changes to instructional strategies. That refinement was actionable and specific, and would put the DTT back on track toward its vision. Like a chef who improves a good recipe by adjusting the ingredients after he has successfully made it once or twice, district leaders must take the initiative to improve their practice of CSI by making ongoing refinements.

Reflecting and Refining in Action

In the pages that follow, we will return to the three case study districts that we have tracked throughout this book, focusing now on the progress they experienced after taking time to reflect on the school improvement work in their districts. We will watch how they made discoveries that initially seemed minor but allowed them to make high-impact adjustments to their plans. A small change early in the course of a flight makes a big difference in where the plane lands. Each of these three districts has taken steps to refine the work and ensure long-term, scalable improvement efforts, while maintaining a focus on the outcome of CSI—improving teaching and learning.

By looking deeper into the case study districts, we will also see how different transformation teams—alongside executive district leadership and outside experts—approach the task of being reflective to inform their future work.

Evansville Vanderburgh School Corporation

In Evansville, where all schools in the district are engaging in data-driven inquiry, continuous reflection and refinement have become part of the culture of the district and are embedded in "the Evansville way." Alongside the DTT, school transformation teams have discovered the value of the reflection and refinement process as they have incorporated it into their team functioning.

At the conclusion of its second year of CSI, the DTT in Evansville was pleased to see that some school teams were making dramatic progress in the work. These teams had garnered whole-school decision making through engaging in the inquiry cycle, and teachers throughout these buildings had developed a strong understanding of the steps of Data Wise.[1] However, other schools had experienced significant challenges and had not been as successful. What was the difference? The DTT realized it needed to dig into the data to find answers.

By engaging in thoughtful discussions with STTs about successes and challenges, the DTT set out to determine how it could refine school improvement efforts to maximize each school's results from the inquiry process. In their conversations with transformation teams, and after reflecting on what happened from their own vantage point, the DTT members discovered three key components in the more successful schools: tailored support, informal leadership, and direct instructional improvements. These elements offered an answer to their question of why some schools experienced more challenges than others when implementing the inquiry cycle. With this in mind, the DTT thought through making refinements in these areas of difference:

- *Tailored support.* Different schools need different support—it sounds obvious, but it's harder to put into practice. The DTT found that some schools needed continued support to implement the inquiry cycle with fidelity, while other schools were ready to move the work down to departments and grade-level teams.
- *Informal leadership.* The DTT noticed that schools experiencing success had informal teacher leaders who engaged teachers across a whole building in the work of inquiry and data-driven decision making. These leaders ensured that the whole faculty—not just select pockets—improved its practice.

- *Instructional improvement.* As described in the vignette to this chapter, not all schools in Evansville were experiencing the same levels of success. In addition to lacking informal leadership, many of the struggling schools had created action plans that neglected to have a direct impact on instruction.

Focusing on these three areas, the DTT set out to determine how to refine its work. From their reflection, the team members realized that they would need to provide relevant, timely support tailored to schools' changing needs. Schools needed the DTT's support regardless of where they were in the school improvement process.

To discern which support was most relevant for each school, the DTT carefully considered the school's status and needs in three areas: 1) the school's level of success with implementing the inquiry cycle, 2) the STT's understanding of the cycle and ability to lead the school in improvement efforts, and 3) the school's level of ownership for the process. After looking at these areas in relation to each school, the DTT noticed that some schools were ready to take the inquiry process to the next level, while others needed assistance just making it from step to step within the inquiry process. Accordingly, the DTT prepared to deliver specialized support for this range of needs across schools.

Some schools needed the district's support in taking the inquiry process to the next level: they'd done well with the first stages of implementation and were ready to further refine improvement efforts. These schools expressed a desire to move the inquiry work from a whole-school process to one that would happen in individual grade levels and/or department teams. The DTT knew that meeting this challenge was possible because the schools had thrived in their implementation of the process in the prior year. STTs at these schools had truly involved their entire faculties in the work and, as a result, the number of individuals who were capable of leading the work had grown. The DTT was able to support these schools in moving to the next level by offering relevant professional development and specific, actionable feedback.

Other schools needed assistance just getting from step to step within the inquiry process. These schools showed pockets of promise where teachers were making changes, but they didn't achieve success in schoolwide implementation of the inquiry cycle. Predictably, their measurable results in student outcomes and instructional strategies were lower than other schools. To provide tailored support to these schools, the DTT members had their work cut out for them. They first crafted relevant PD that reinforced the inquiry cycle's importance and process. Then, their more difficult quest was to figure out how to encourage schoolwide

participation. Here they applied ideas from successful schools to refine their strategies: they realized that all schools needed the enthusiasm and guidance of informal teacher leaders. These teachers worked with STTs to encourage whole-faculty
ownership in the process, and they mentored teachers who needed extra assistance.

The DTT's quest, then, was to create a similar cadre of teachers at all schools.
Through reflection, the DTT refined its efforts, shifting its attention from providing
support in the steps of the Data Wise Improvement Process itself to instead supporting the development of informal teacher leaders in each building who would
push the work down into grade- and department-level teams. The DTT knew that
for CSI to truly impact every classroom, it had to originate from teacher leaders
intimately involved in the work at the classroom level. Top-down initiatives—even
from STTs—would have little impact without grassroots ownership. The DTT
envisioned teachers filling these roles across all schools in the district. Knowing
that they could not rely solely on the formal roles set forth within CSI, the DTT
members explored ways to cultivate informal leadership. They realized that serving
on the STT had developed many teacher leaders the previous year and wondered
if rotating STT members would provide an additional opportunity to promote
informal teacher leadership across a faculty. With this outcome in mind, the DTT
approached several schools with this recommendation for strengthening the STTs'
work. School leaders rotated team members, exposing more teachers to opportunities for leadership. With district encouragement and support—and championed by
their colleague teachers who had previously served on the team—these new teacher
leaders were poised to have a big impact.

The final issue was a big one: how could the DTT better assist school teams in
focusing more intently on instruction? As the DTT reviewed school action plans
with a reflecting and refining lens, it noticed a commonality among many teams
that struggled to generate improvements in learning. Action plans at these schools
pointed to students, not teachers, as the solutions. For example, at one school in
Evansville, the solution to improve students' abilities in problem solving was to
create a problem-solving checklist for students to use on their homework and other
assignments.

Of course, creating a problem-solving checklist is not an inherently *bad* idea.
Students could likely benefit from such a tool. What's problematic is that addressing only the student component of the instructional core leads to minimal changes
in learning. Determined to make amends for its insufficient partnership, the DTT
made a concrete commitment to review action plans in the coming year with a
laser focus on the instructional core. It also conceived of a case study activity at

the upcoming training session to help STTs identify the difference between action plans that address all three components of the instructional core and those that address only one.

By examining the existing structure of support that it provided to schools and reflecting on the successes and shortcomings of this structure, the district transformation team at EVSC was able to identify specific refinements that it could make in its work. Through these refinements, the DTT provided more school-specific support, working to build internal capacity across all schools in the district.

Chandler Unified School District

At the end of their first year of implementing CSI in Chandler, school transformation teams and district leaders were acutely aware of the need to refine their implementation of the chosen inquiry cycle (the Data Wise Improvement Process) in order to ensure that efforts in the coming years would be as successful as possible. Realizing that not all schools in the cohort had experienced the same level of growth in student achievement after implementing the cycle, the DTT took time to reflect on the work that individual school teams had done. The team knew that reflection was a powerful tool for reinforcing things that went well and motivating change in areas that didn't go as well. So it decided to support its busy STTs by providing an opportunity for team reflection and refinement alongside the DTT. By sharing this experience, the DTT members could connect better with their school teams; by being privy to the reasoning behind the refinements that school teams planned to make, the DTT would be well positioned to offer relevant support in those endeavors.

In the final session of the year, the DTT led the STTs in a Plus/Delta Protocol (see a portion of the results in table 8.1), which it designed to encourage conversations about what had worked and what hadn't. The DTT was excited to note that all schools were celebrating some level of success, and interested to hear how the teams reflected on elements of the process that had not been as successful.

In this meeting, the DTT took note of comments from school teams, such as "I don't get it. We did all of the steps of the cycle, and we still didn't see the growth that we wanted to," and "I think the main issue is that we focused too much on identifying the learning problem, but not enough on modeling the instructional strategy to teachers so that they could implement it with fidelity." From these insights, the DTT identified a common obstacle for some teams. In focusing intently on learning each step of the cycle, they had lost sight of the desired outcome: improved teaching and learning.

TABLE 8.1

PLUS/DELTA PROTOCOL EXAMPLE

+ *What we did best this year*	Δ *Challenges—things we need to change in the future*
+ Buy-in—all teachers were on board and actively involved. + Our team worked well together. + We used collaboration and innovation to get/keep all teachers involved. + We used our time together effectively.	Δ We (the team) focused too much on teaching our staff the Data Wise process. Δ When we spent time teaching the steps of DW, teachers were sometimes confused—they need to know the "what" and "how" more than the "why." Δ Need to use "whole staff" time more effectively next year.

Source: Chandler Unified School District, Chandler, Arizona

As STTs found out, "being good at Data Wise" wasn't enough to effect the desired changes in teaching and learning. However, losing sight of the forest for the trees did not signal a lack of effort on the STTs' part. In fact, it illustrated the intense focus that teams maintained on learning each step of the inquiry cycle. The DTT used this knowledge to inform its future support of teams, recognizing that training sessions must balance support for the steps of the process alongside a focus on the outcome: improved teaching and learning.

After reflecting with STTs, the DTT was able to guide the schools in making decisions about refining their work to make it more effective. For the STTs in Chandler, this meant looking over what hadn't gone well and engaging in conversations about the challenges they had faced. The school teams that had focused on process over outcome identified several ways they could refine their work to ensure that this was not an issue in coming years. Some of the refinements that one school identified are illustrated in table 8.2.

Meanwhile, reflection by the DTT in Chandler resulted in dramatic changes in the DTT's structure in year two. District instructional and professional development specialists replaced principals. This change linked the instructional resources in the district more closely with the improvement work in which schools engaged, bringing increased support to school teams in areas where they needed it most.

School teams improved also. In the second year of CSI, cohort-one STTs were more efficient and focused. "More time" was no longer the most frequent retort to

TABLE 8.2

CHANDLER MIDDLE SCHOOL REFINEMENTS TO THE PROCESS

What we did this year	What we'll do next year
Spent too much time learning the steps of Data Wise and trying to teach them to our staff.	Focus on the outcome—improving teaching and learning.
Spent too long looking at quantitative data to inform decision making.	Focus more on looking at *both* quantitative and qualitative data to ensure that we're identifying a root cause.
Spent too much time trying to engage staff in every step of the Data Wise process.	Make high-level decisions, present them to the staff members, and ask for their input in making the decisions that will impact their teaching.
Presented too many options for staff to choose from.	Focus on narrowing down the options, getting feedback from staff members, and planning in response to their feedback.

Source: Chandler Unified School District, Chandler, Arizona

"how can we help?" questions from the DTT. Instead, teams asked for ideas, support, coaching, and sharing among teams. And as for focus, at the first training session of the second year, the teams could hardly be interrupted with lunch. Half the teams ordered food into the district office so they wouldn't lose the focus and trajectory they had gained in their team time prior to lunch.

Ending the year with this practice of reflecting and refining equipped all transformation teams to start the next cycle of data-driven inquiry with a renewed focus on the outcome over the process, and a better understanding of their roles in leading the improvement efforts.

Portland Public Schools

Through four years of engaging in CSI, the DTT in Portland embraced the practice of reflecting and refining. This way of doing business was becoming the norm. In fact, Portland DTT members reflected at the conclusion of every training session and more extensively at the end of each cohort year.

After training sessions, the DTT, Nike School Innovation Fund, and outside experts immediately reflected on the successes, challenges, and ideas for refinements for the future. The immediacy of the reflection proved important—the team found that memories fade quickly, and it makes sense to capture the collective group's thinking as soon after a session as possible. Figure 8.1 demonstrates an example of a post-session debrief and reflection session in Portland.

After each year, the district transformation team took an entire day to reflect on and refine the year's work. Beyond the scope of the post-session debriefs, this end-of-year time was intentionally designed to amplify the DTT's overall work in relation to the work of the STTs. To lead these holistic reflection and refinement meetings, PPS, in conjunction with its outside provider, created a discussion guide named the Keep, Tweak, Rethink (K-T-R) model. This model guided conversations and ensured that the practice of reflecting and refining remained at the heart of the meetings. With the structure, individuals were encouraged to categorize practices as 1) successful—*keep* in place in the future, 2) moderately successful—alter slightly to better meet the district's needs (*tweak*), and 3) ineffective—completely *rethink*. Figure 8.2 shows an excerpt from one of these meetings that illustrates the K-T-R model.

Over the years, the Portland DTT, in collaboration with the Nike School Innovation Fund and the outside providers, has made the following key enhancements to its program: each has yielded exciting results. Many other enhancements have also been made, but these four stick out as particularly important learning for other districts.

- Aligned the School Improvement Plan template with the inquiry cycle
- Took over ownership for the training sessions from the outside provider
- Empowered regional administrators to provide feedback and coaching to schools on the inquiry process
- Used independent evaluation as a tool for initiative improvement and to ensure a continued focus of the work on student achievement

School Improvement Plan alignment

After early inquiry implementers wondered how the CSI work fit into other district improvement processes, such as the yearly School Improvement Plans (SIPs), the DTT was determined to create more alignment. As DTT members investigated, they realized two levels of revisions were required, and they set a plan in motion to complete the work thoughtfully over an eighteen-month period.

First, the DTT needed to align the language used on the SIP with the language from Portland's chosen inquiry cycle. As an example, the SIP required schools to identify an area of weakness, whereas the inquiry cycle divided that category into weaknesses among learners and among practitioners. Separating the SIP column

FIGURE 8.1

PPS POST-SESSION DEBRIEF AND REFLECTION

Date of session: August 25, 2010   *Time:* 11:00 a.m.–3:00 p.m.   *Location:* Freedom School
Participants: Cohort 4 principals and NSIF leadership team

Session objectives:

1. Provide overview of the program: goals, team expectations, and supports and resources available to schools.

2. Discuss principals' roles in the NSIF PLC to enable them to be more effective leaders of the process.

3. Introduce principals to the Data Wise process.

4. Provide school leaders with a plan to begin creating a culture of inquiry within their schools.

5. Begin a dialogue about how schools can use student assessment data to improve instruction.

6. Introduce the use of protocols to "promote participation, ensure equity, and build trust" (*The Power of Protocols*).

7. Prepare principals for the next steps in the process.

Successful components	Challenges	Refinements for the future
Agenda and objectives were clear and easy to follow.		Send agenda and objectives to participants prior to the session so that they can be thinking ahead about the session.
	Constructing the improvement process.	Give participants more details to guide them in completing this activity.
Student writing samples gave participants a clear picture of students' ability levels.		Consider providing additional writing samples to give participants more to look at/analyze. Provide an exemplar paper.
	Writing samples were not coded by ethnicity and gender—some people were interested in knowing more about the students.	Code the writing samples (gender, ethnicity, SpEd, ELL, etc.).
Protocol for looking at student work was successful (Slice writing protocol).		Provide participants with a hard copy of the protocol—many requested this so that they could use the protocol at their schools.
	Data Collection Template was unclear.	Make changes to the template so that it aligns with SIP language. For example, rather than referring to "short-, medium-, and long-term" assessments, refer to assessments by name (benchmark, OAKS, etc.).

Source: Portland Public Schools, Portland, Oregon

FIGURE 8.2

NOTES FROM AN END-OF-YEAR REFLECTION SESSION

PPS End-of-Year Debrief

Date: May 2010

Participants: PPS DTT members, NSIF leaders, Education Direction team members

Purpose of meeting:
- To reflect on the NSIF PLC work that has been done this year, noting areas of success and challenges that we have faced
- To make plans for refining the work to make it more effective

Keep, Tweak, Rethink

Keep: Elements of the work that we feel were successful this year that we would like to implement again next year

Tweak: Elements of the work that need to be altered slightly to make them more effective next year

Rethink: Elements of the work that need to be completely rethought for successful implementation next year

Keep	*Tweak*	*Rethink*
Focus on innovation.	Process for identifying learning problems—need to alter current elements of effective LCPs to include the following: ■ Must identify an achievement gap. ■ Schools must disaggregate student data to show performance by ethnic subgroups.	Different objectives for principals (are there things that we want principals to know and be able to do outside of the objectives that we have for other school transformation team members?).
Continue to use current writing framework and district writing binders as the foundations for effective writing instruction.	Schools must choose to implement an instructional strategy that addresses the achievement gap.	How the PLC, Data Wise, and other district initiatives fit together.
Pre and post surveys at the school level.		How to provide better support to schools between sessions.
Pre and post surveys for leadership teams		

Source: Portland Public Schools, Portland, Oregon

into two columns and renaming them "learner-centered problem" and "problem of practice" (Data Wise Improvement Process terms) erased all confusion among STTs about what the SIP was asking for. The added benefit was the increase in general alignment within the district. Schools really took note of the DTT's efforts to streamline and align the work within the district.

Next, the DTT needed to create a process that schools would follow to complete their SIPs prior to submitting them to the DTT. In Portland, as in many other districts, the SIP was typically completed by the principal, with minimal input from the rest of the school community. The inquiry cycle again guided the creation of a set of guidelines for schools to complete their SIPs, which encouraged effective team collaboration, whole-school decision making, and many other practices described in this book.

Ownership for training sessions

At the onset of the work in Portland, the outside expert was able to design and execute effective trainings based on the experience he had garnered elsewhere. Portland was determined, however, to take over the work of planning and presenting training sessions, even though its experience with the inquiry cycle was limited to its locale.

The results of the gradual release from outside experts to DTT couldn't have been planned or executed any more effectively. DTT members regularly comment on their increased feelings of professional satisfaction, and the outside experts even feel more helpful as a resource during planning and presenting, not as the main show. Taking the attention away from the outside provider has also given school teams a stronger sense of ownership of the work, as DTT members have existing relationships with the schools and are able to tailor the message to fit Portland's context and history.

Regional administrator role

Once the DTT came to grips with the fact that regional administrators (RAs) were not being leveraged effectively in regular interactions with principals, for providing feedback, or holding schools accountable for things such as SIPs, the team's wheels started turning. The DTT recognized the untapped value of the RAs' roles in the inquiry cycle. The plain truth was that RAs wanted to participate and help; they believed in the CSI work. However, RAs felt disconnected and separate from the DTT.

The call for RAs throughout the district to become more knowledgeable about CSI practices—and, in turn, more supportive of the schools engaging in data-driven inquiry—has been happily accepted. The DTT has enlisted RAs to attend the district training sessions and engage in additional conversations and training with the outside experts in order to increase their understanding of the inquiry process. By learning more about the inquiry cycle that is driving the work of improvement at the school level, the RAs can provide timely and relevant feedback to schools as they submit their SIPs for review. In addition, at the DTT's recommendation, the RAs have engaged principals in monthly support calls—a practice that has built each RA's understanding of the work that schools are doing and creates stronger partnerships between district leaders and school leaders. By seeking further involvement from the RAs, the DTT hopes to ensure alignment of initiatives and to provide support and accountability to the schools engaging in CSI.

Independent evaluation and focus on student achievement

Portland, with coaching from the Nike School Innovation Fund, vigilantly tracked the progress of the training sessions, the work of the school teams, and the changes happening throughout school buildings. The district accomplished this by bringing on an unbiased, third-party evaluator who took the objectives of the program and created a robust measurement system to track progress against the key objectives.

Thanks in part to all this measurement, Portland keeps its eyes on the end goal: improving student learning. And especially thanks to the Nike School Innovation Fund's insistence on maintaining a laser focus on that end goal, the outside evaluator tracks student learning regularly, alongside other measures of leadership, team functioning, and school culture. The learning in Portland is simple: measure what matters, and give results to key stakeholders to make adjustments to the plan in order to achieve those core objectives.

CONCLUSION

As an integral practice of CSI, reflecting and refining requires that districts regularly engage in collaborative conversations about the work that is being done both at the district and school levels. As we can see from the districts' experiences, this practice benefits all who are involved. From planning for the future to making immediate changes that impact day-to-day efforts, reflecting and refining comprise some of the most important practices of Collaborative School Improvement.

As the culminating practice, reflecting and refining are intricately connected to the seven other CSI practices that we've explored in this book. From identifying an inquiry cycle to leveraging expertise, the DTT can improve each practice by taking the time to reflect on its implementation and by making refinements that increase efficiency. The art of reflection informs all of the other practices, and it provides valuable insight to leaders as they refine the work of CSI.

■

TAKEAWAYS

- *Win-win: all stakeholders benefit from the practice of reflecting and refining.* When districts take the time to reflect on the work that they have done (both at the district level and within schools), all stakeholders benefit. District transformation teams gain insight into the work that is being done at the school level, and school transformation teams learn how they can tweak their work to make inquiry-based improvement efforts as successful as possible.
- *A mirror is only good for showing what is happening now: reflection must be timely—this practice is not effective if teams let long periods of time pass before they engage in it.* Transformation teams should devote time (both during and at the end of the cycle) to reflect on the work that has been done. By engaging in this practice in a timely manner (and not waiting months or years to consider successes and challenges), teams are better positioned to refine school improvement efforts.
- *We are never too old to learn: reflecting and refining inform each of the other seven practices of CSI.* Regardless of how long your district has been engaging in CSI, each practice you implement has the potential to be more effective when you take the time to reflect and refine. Examples from DTTs we have worked with (and chronicled throughout this book) show how this practice can positively impact school improvement efforts at all stages and through each practice.

CHAPTER 9

Implementing the Practices of CSI
Chandler's First Three Years

Gina Vukovich, a former principal and current Director of Assessment and Federal Programs in the Chandler Unified School District (CUSD), sat at her desk wondering if she could actually make it happen. She was reviewing her notes and thinking through the incredible insights she and several principals had gained while attending the Data Wise Institute at the Harvard Graduate School of Education (HGSE). Unlike many improvement efforts she'd studied, she felt that this one from the conference had real merit—it could actually work. It could drive sustainable, inquiry-based improvement in teaching and learning at all schools in her district. In fact, it was for this very reason that Camille Casteel and Susan Eissinger—Chandler's superintendent and assistant superintendent, respectively—had agreed to send the team to Harvard, and the impetus for their encouragement and support for Gina as she returned motivated to make a difference.

Gina knew that implementing an inquiry cycle would help schools develop a collaborative culture of data-informed decision making. Experience had shown that classroom instruction was the greatest lever for school improvement, and she knew that inquiry cycles could positively impact classroom practice. The vision put butterflies in her stomach, and she knew her team was onto something big. It wouldn't be easy—that she knew for certain. Gina speculated about how to structure inquiry-based school improvement in Chandler as a process rather than an isolated initiative. There was the problem, too, of scope: as a seasoned administrator, she and other district leaders often wondered how to help more than just a handful of schools improve teaching and learning in their buildings. She had noticed that districtwide improvement efforts of the past had predictably worked well in corners of her district, but hadn't returned results across all the schools. What would it take to apply the strategies she'd learned at the conference to her district on a grand scale?

Throughout this book, we have highlighted the practices of Collaborative School Improvement by discussing the work of three separate—and very different—districts. In this chapter, we will zoom in on CUSD and watch how it brought the whole process to life. We'll attempt to paint a clear picture of Chandler's three-year journey toward fully embracing CSI to improve teaching and learning across all of its schools. By tracing the work of district lead Gina Vukovich and her district transformation team, we hope to offer a clear road map for how districts can partner with schools to effectively implement an inquiry-based cycle for improving teaching and learning districtwide.

In the following pages, we will recount Chandler's journey, which began nearly a year before the district engaged its first group of schools in the program. We'll mention the work of the key players involved in making CSI successful over these three years: district leaders, the DTT, the outside experts, and the schools engaging in the inquiry cycle. Then we'll conclude with a snapshot of the district as it begins to engage a second cohort of schools in the inquiry cycle that it has adopted. Chandler's story is not intended to serve as an all-inclusive guide to implementing CSI in your district, but it will offer a wealth of practical information on logistics and possible applications. Figures 9.1, 9.2, and 9.3, which are timelines for Chandler's implementation, provide concrete dates and events that coincide with the more detailed descriptions in the paragraphs that follow each figure.

GETTING STARTED: YEAR ONE

Summer 2009

After returning from the HGSE Data Wise Institute, Gina and her colleagues—three junior high school principals—knew they were onto something big. The Data Wise Improvement Process they studied was different from other school improvement programs they'd encountered previously: instead of making short-term adjustments via district-mandated programs, Data Wise was a process for discovering and supporting the district's highest-priority needs. It was just what their district needed to break out of years of stalled student progress.[1]

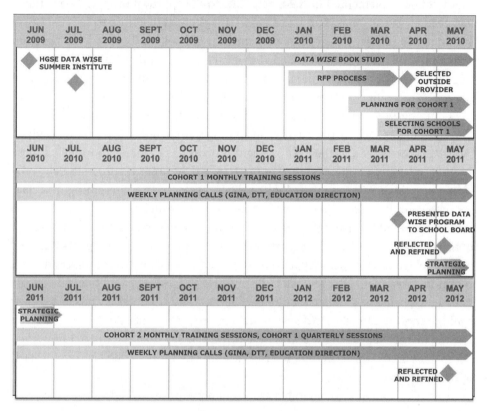

CHANDLER IMPLEMENTATION CALENDAR 2009–2012

After carefully preparing, Gina's team presented the Data Wise Improvement Process and the program they proposed to implement in Chandler to Susan and Camille. They reviewed stagnant test scores from the past few years, and noted that instruction was likely not improving sufficiently to drive improvements in student learning. Though their district was relatively high performing, they showed how it could benefit from the Data Wise Improvement Process, which would provide a structure for schools to dig down to the level of student data and generate changes to instruction that would impact the instructional core. Though they first proposed implementing Data Wise in a select group of participating schools, Gina and her colleagues felt that this process could have an even greater impact if they could bring it to scale.

Susan and Camille, seeing their hopes come to fruition, threw their weight behind the proposal, and Gina began making plans. Knowing that the program could not be implemented immediately (due to the approval process, board funding, need to find an outside provider, etc.), Gina decided that the best way to inform and motivate district leaders was by launching a book study about the program with all CUSD principals. Gina hoped that this type of study would allow her colleagues to experience what she had learned at Harvard, and she felt confident that she could light a fire of interest throughout the district.

Beginning in November 2009, Gina and her colleagues planned monthly sessions (ending in May 2010) to gather all administrators in the district for a study of the *Data Wise* book and the improvement process itself. The team modeled these sessions after those it had attended at the Harvard Summer Institute, thereby providing principals with an inside look at the inquiry process. Presenting in a clear and engaging manner, Gina's team covered the tools and protocols that schools could implement to ensure that they were using all types of data to inform instruction. To facilitate real-time understanding, the book-study participants engaged in a sample inquiry cycle: they used district data to guide conversations and build common assessment literacy. After testing the process even in this small-scale sample, the principals understood Gina's, Susan's, and Camille's enthusiasm—they could see how inquiry-based decision making brought results. And, even though it was the district suggesting the work, the principals saw that the district preserved school autonomy, while simultaneously carving out a more effective role for itself in school improvement.

In April 2010, Gina collaborated with inquiry experts to lead an informational session that gave administrators a clear idea of what the adopted inquiry cycle would look like when implemented in schools. Gina's hours of preparation paid off: this session sparked interest in a number of school administrators, and became the starting point for the application process that schools would go through to be considered for participation in CUSD's pilot implementation of the inquiry cycle.

Winter 2010

With the book study successfully underway, Gina began planning for the implementation of the inquiry cycle in Chandler. To ensure success with such an enormous project, Gina began searching for an outside provider who would best meet the district's needs. She knew that the district would need an expert to facilitate the training sessions for participating schools—someone who had been through the process and could coach her district through the details. Based on district standards, Gina was required to start a Request for Proposal (RFP) process (a requirement for any vendor services over $30,000); in early January 2010, Gina issued an RFP for a "Facilitator for Inquiry-Based District and School Improvement Initiative." This RFP required interested parties to create a scope for the work, estimate deliverables, present qualifications, and quote cost (among other things). It also enabled the DTT to gauge the outside experts' levels of expertise in facilitating professional development, and specifically in supporting inquiry-based school improvement throughout a large district.

After receiving multiple RFP responses, Gina and the district team narrowed the field of applicants based on the criteria they had established. In April 2010, they selected an outside provider who had solid experience in each of those areas and could meet the district's needs.[2] This partnership was a big deal for Gina: she knew that the right experts would make all the difference in her ability to achieve her goal of improving teaching and learning in Chandler. Excited to begin the journey, Gina and the outside experts began planning to launch the district's pilot implementation of the inquiry cycle in June 2010. This preparation process required identifying a district lead, building a DTT, selecting schools to participate, and generating a yearlong plan for the program.

Selecting a district lead

Knowing that the district's efforts to partner with schools would be most successful if one individual served as a leader, Gina naturally took on the role of district lead. She stood with the support of her colleagues and executive district leadership—especially Susan and Camille. In this role, Gina operated as the primary communicator between the DTT and the outside provider, as well as between the DTT and the schools. Having attended the HGSE Data Wise Institute and led the book study, Gina's strong foundational knowledge of the Data Wise Improvement Process made her the best choice for this role. In addition, her excitement about CSI and her genuine belief in the potential that it had to impact the district strengthened her qualifications.

Selecting a district transformation team

In planning for the first year of CSI in Chandler, Gina was excited to build her team. She recognized the need to organize a team that could support participating schools in the implementation of the inquiry cycle. Because she didn't have any previous experience leading this type of team, Gina relied on input from the outside experts, whose experiences with other districts offered valuable insight into selecting the individuals who would serve on the first Chandler DTT.

With the support of district executive leadership and the outside provider, Gina determined that this DTT could do two things at once: it would not only support schools in the implementation of Data Wise, but it would also use the inquiry process to examine the bigger assessment issues that were plaguing the district and inhibiting the use of data to inform improvement efforts. With these goals in mind, Susan and Gina selected team members—primarily district principals—who they knew could offer insight into the districtwide assessment system, and who had administrative experience. With her team by her side, Gina now tackled the process of deciding which schools should participate. Gina knew these principals would be great partners throughout the process, but she still sometimes had to catch her breath at the magnitude of their shared undertaking. Her commitment was strong, and excitement was still evident in her voice, but she felt sober, too, about bringing to life the changes she'd dreamed of. Taking a deep breath, she moved confidently forward in planning for the future.

Spring 2010

Selecting schools to participate in the program

The DTT knew that the method it used to select schools to participate in the first year of inquiry was of utmost importance. Attentive to district resources, the team members realized that if they involved all schools at once, the district's time, funding, and physical space to hold sessions would be stretched too thin. Alternatively, if they took a multicohort approach—working with a small cohort of schools as a pilot group in year one of implementation—they could be more responsible with the district's resource budget. Based on their long-term vision, the DTT members knew that all schools would eventually be involved in subsequent years of the program, so they decided to work with the multicohort approach. But which schools should they involve in the first cohort? The team determined that the best way to engage a pilot group of schools in the inquiry cycle would be to have them submit an application expressing interest in the program and confirming that they understood the process and the time commitments that it would require.

To call for applications, the DTT worked with the outside provider to craft a letter that was sent to all school principals, outlining the project, participation commitments, and opportunities and challenges associated with the program. This

---

BOX 9.1

PARTICIPATION REQUIREMENTS

Participation requires the following commitments:

- Maintain a transformation team, consisting of five to eight teachers and administrators, including the principal.
- Convene the transformation team for (roughly) monthly daylong working seminars away from the school, and periodic out-of-contract time (reimbursed for time).
- Convene the transformation team for monthly afterschool meetings at the school.
- Utilize several district PD days to support this work.
- Engage the entire faculty in key protocols during faculty meeting time.
- Follow through on the basic principles of each step of the Data Wise process.
- Participate in monthly phone calls (principals only) with project leaders.
- Embody a desire to do "whatever it takes" to dramatically improve student learning.

---

letter also explained the nomination process, which required that the project be introduced to faculty members, who then had to agree to the stated commitments, as shown in box 9.1. In addition, the letter listed the nomination questions that a group of teacher leaders (named by the principal) would need to answer in order to be considered for participation.

Upon receiving the applications from interested schools, the DTT reviewed each carefully and determined which schools would be best suited to participate in year one of the inquiry process. These schools received a letter of acceptance, which welcomed them to the cohort and provided guidelines for school leaders to use when selecting the members of their transformation teams. These guidelines, as written in the letter of acceptance, are illustrated in box 9.2. After the school transformation teams were formed, the DTT requested a list of team members, their roles, and their contact information (for use in future correspondence).

Planning for cohort one
Following the initial set-up stage for implementing CSI in Chandler, the DTT began collaborating closely with the outside experts to facilitate the Data Wise

---

BOX 9.2

GUIDELINES FOR SELECTING SCHOOL TEAMS

Please choose five to eight additional members of your transformation team (the transformation team size can range from five to nine total people, which includes you, the principal). Consider the following when selecting your transformation team members.

- **The number of transformation team members should be related to your school size**. Small schools (five hundred to seven hundred students) should consider forming transformation teams that range from five to six members. Medium-size schools (seven hundred to one thousand students) should consider forming transformation teams that range from six to seven members. Large schools (more than one thousand students) should consider forming transformation teams that range from seven to nine members. Some smaller schools might be tempted to form transformation teams of nine, to "share" the professional development opportunity with more people. However, experience has shown that smaller transformation teams are able to accomplish more in a given amount of time. You know your school best, so we trust your personal judgment of how many members you should include in your team, within the ranges provided above.

- **Please consider including members of your transformation team who represent the diversity in your students and staff**. Members with different ethnicities, ages, and genders will enable your transformation team to be innovative and consider critical decisions from multiple points of view.

- **Be sure that various grade levels and content departments are represented in your transformation team**. For elementary schools, ensure that you have transformation team members from at least three grade levels. For middle and high schools, ensure that all core academic departments are represented, as well as multiple grade levels.

- **Finally, consider the personality of transformation team members**. An ideal transformation team member is one who is open to becoming an informal teacher leader and can gain credibility among fellow teachers because of his or her known hard work and effort. He or she is also open to trying new things and encouraging fellow teachers to try things that might be out of their comfort zone.

Improvement Process. With key CSI players and leaders in place for a group of eleven schools, the DTT and the outside experts fastened their seatbelts and began planning for the year.

Their first task was to outline scope. A section of the RFP that the outside provider had submitted included a proposed scope for the implementation of the Data Wise inquiry cycle (see exhibit 9.1 at the end of this chapter). This scope served as an excellent starting point. From there, district leaders detailed when schools would go through the inquiry cycle and what its final implementation would look like in Chandler.

Next, the DTT sat down with the district calendar in hand to determine its plan for implementing the Data Wise Improvement Process in year one. The team knew that if this work was going to be successful, it must fit into the existing structure of the school calendar. With a modified year-round district calendar (providing 180 days of instruction), district leaders had to consider dates that would be best for training sessions, but they also had to be mindful of state and district testing schedules and vacation time. They scheduled dates when STTs would most likely be available to engage in planning time at their buildings. They also planned dates for monthly training sessions that covered one step of the inquiry cycle at a time, and ensured that teams had time to take the process back to their schools and implement it with fidelity. By leveraging the expertise of the outside provider, Gina and her team were able to create a plan that followed the step-by-step inquiry cycle presented in *Data Wise*, and that fit perfectly into the modified year-round school calendar already in place.

The early creation of this calendar was integral for two reasons. First, it allowed Gina—who was serving as the primary liaison between the district and the STTs—to reserve the dates and meeting locations early enough that few scheduling conflicts would occur. Second, by having the dates on the calendar, Gina could inform the participating schools when they would be expected to attend sessions; this information was extremely valuable to the schools as they worked to create their own calendars.

Once this calendar was approved, Gina then sent it on to the participating schools so that they could begin reserving dates on their individual calendars—both for time to be spent away from their buildings in training sessions, and also for time that they would need for planning and preparation between sessions. In addition to the district calendar outlining the dates and times of training sessions,

Gina and the outside experts created a timeline template to aid the STTs in setting aside the time they would need to devote to the inquiry process between sessions. This template (see exhibit 9.2 at the end of this chapter) gave STTs more specific guidelines regarding time commitments and expectations. Many schools remarked that this tool proved very helpful as they planned their work for the year.

Finally, Gina and the outside experts also generated a big-picture project timeline, which documented when certain steps in the planning process would be completed. This calendar provided a detailed outline of work steps (for both the DTT and the outside experts) and served the purpose of holding all parties accountable for having work completed well in advance. It also offered the district executive leadership an overview of the work that was taking place. Included in this calendar were dates for training sessions, times for planning calls between the outside experts and district lead, and dates for the submission of work (agendas, presentations, documents for printing, etc.). By creating this document ahead of time and agreeing on the timeline, all parties were aware of expectations and responsibilities.

YEAR TWO: IMPLEMENTING SCHOOL-BASED INQUIRY CYCLES

Summer 2010

Year one of the school-based implementation of the adopted inquiry cycle in Chandler started off according to schedule. Having laid a strong foundation for the work by investing serious planning time, the DTT was ready to partner with the eleven participating schools in the implementation of the adopted inquiry cycle.

FIGURE 9.2

CHANDLER IMPLEMENTATION CALENDAR 2010–2011

JUN 2010	JUL 2010	AUG 2010	SEPT 2010	OCT 2010	NOV 2010	DEC 2010	JAN 2011	FEB 2011	MAR 2011	APR 2011	MAY 2011
COHORT 1 MONTHLY TRAINING SESSIONS											
WEEKLY PLANNING CALLS (GINA, DTT, EDUCATION DIRECTION)											
										PRESENTED DATA WISE PROGRAM TO SCHOOL BOARD	
									REFLECTED AND REFINED		
										STRATEGIC PLANNING	

Rather than inviting the school teams to simply show up at the monthly training sessions without any preparation, Gina proactively supplied them with useful information prior to each session. To support the schools participating in cohort one, Gina created a protocol for disseminating information to STTs. One week prior to each training session, Gina made it her practice to send the teams all relevant information about the upcoming session. In an email to each participating school's principal, Gina outlined the preparation that STTs would need to do prior to the session. Gina assigned them to read chapters from *Data Wise*, engage their whole staff in planning meetings, and perform other relevant session preparation. Her message also included the objectives for the session, the agenda, and other important logistical information such as the time and location of the training session.

Over the course of the year, it became obvious that Gina needed to refine her communication technique to ensure that all members of the STTs were receiving the information on time. Initially, Gina simply sent these messages to the school principals and relied on them to pass on the information to their teams. However, the information occasionally got delayed because school principals were dealing with many demands simultaneously. In response, Gina determined that a more effective (and efficient) way to communicate information to the STT members was to email each directly. While it took more work up front to gather each person's current email address, this modification to Gina's communication plan with participating schools proved very helpful in ensuring that everyone was prepared for the meetings. In fact, her method of emailing everyone involved became the standard practice in the following year.

After the first session, schools indicated that they wanted (and needed) electronic versions of all of the documents that were used during the session. Responding to this need, Gina coordinated with the outside provider to ensure that all materials (presentations, agendas, templates, protocols, etc.) were sent to the teams prior to the start of the session. With these documents ready to go, many school teams were able to start working on their planning and next steps during the team time that was provided at the session. Rather than using the old method of handwriting notes that later had to be typed into the appropriate templates, teams could input information directly into their templates during the session. They also wasted less session time transferring materials to participants (via email or thumb drives), and therefore had more time to plan efficiently.

To most effectively partner with participating schools, the DTT also worked hard to provide support and resources during and after the sessions. This meant that, during the session, the DTT organized all necessary materials (including laptops that participants could use to access the district data warehouse) and made them available for school teams. The DTT's hard work prior to the session meant that STTs always had what they needed during the session.

The DTT also offered post-session support by providing school teams with feedback and recommendations—a practice that not only helped the teams improve their work, but also held them accountable for completing "homework" assignments. In year one of implementation, Gina and the DTT leveraged the outside provider to review assignments and give feedback. Gina was fully involved in the process, which allowed her to learn more about the steps in the inquiry cycle and prepared her (with the DTT) to take on that role in years to come.

The work that Gina and the district team performed between sessions went beyond providing support and resources to the schools participating in the program. In addition to regularly interacting with school teams, Gina also devoted time to making weekly calls to the outside experts. During these calls, Gina and the experts would speak candidly about successes and challenges both at the sessions and back at the schools, and they would engage in "reflect and refine" conversations, which often led to making changes that allowed Gina to better meet the schools' needs. Modeling the use of effective team practices on these planning calls, Gina and the outside experts religiously followed agendas that they created prior to the call. The outside experts acted as the facilitators of the meetings, taking notes and documenting action items and next steps for all parties involved in the planning process. These weekly calls provided time for connection and reflection, and also kept the outside experts abreast of the happenings within the district.

Providing support before, during, and after training sessions proved to be one of the most valuable aspects of the role that Gina—with support from the DTT—took on as the leader of CSI in Chandler. In addition to ensuring that schools were successfully engaging in the implementation of the inquiry cycle, Gina was building capacity by leveraging the outside provider to regularly interact with, reflect upon, and revise the work that was taking place.

As year one of school-based implementation of the inquiry cycle in Chandler came to a close, the DTT sat down with the outside provider to discuss the future of the CSI project in the district. Satisfied with the work that the first cohort of schools had accomplished, and pleased with how the DTT and the participating schools had approached and addressed the challenges that arose, Gina was determined that Chandler's participation in the CSI project needed to become a districtwide mandate—something that the district had never before attempted.

Planning for Year Two of CSI

In the summer of 2011, the DTT and the outside provider set up a time to discuss the year with Susan and Camille, both of whom were eager to hear the results of the work they had instigated. Like other executive-level leaders in the district, both Camille and Susan wanted to hear about how the work was impacting schools in the district. With pride, Gina presented the data to her colleagues—which showed increases in student proficiency in each of the participating schools—and they engaged in a conversation about how this work could be scaled up in a way that would be sustainable for years to come.

Because of her strong belief in the potential impact that the process could have on all schools within the district—and with encouragement from both Camille and Susan—Gina had presented the idea to the school board again in the spring of 2011. The feedback that Gina and the DTT received from the board members was positive: they, too, felt like the CSI project had the potential to impact both teaching and learning in Chandler. However, school board members had questions about how the implementation of the adopted inquiry cycle could be a long-term, sustainable initiative throughout the district. As a result, they requested that the team create a five-year strategic plan to outline how this work could become a district-wide way of doing business.

Creating the five-year strategic plan signaled the district's commitment to making the CSI project a districtwide, mandated initiative—something way out of the box for a district that had not mandated any initiatives or programs in the past. By creating a plan to engage every school in the district in CSI, Gina and other district leaders were sending a clear message to schools that data-driven inquiry was not transient and could measurably improve teaching and student learning. Pleased with the outcomes from year one, Gina and the team knew that creating a plan for district leaders to partner with schools in school improvement would be the catalyst for long-term, sustainable change across the district. From the perspective of district leaders and the DTT, this plan would not only support the implementation of the inquiry cycle, but it would also aid schools in narrowing their focus on that which mattered the most for teachers and students—improving outcomes.

Creating a plan of that nature requires some serious homework. After weeks of speaking with the stakeholders who had been involved in the first year of the CSI project—the superintendent, associate superintendent, board members, participating STTs, and the outside experts—Gina led the DTT in finalizing a strategic plan to submit to the school board (for an excerpt of this plan, see exhibit 9.3 at the end of this chapter). This strategic plan clearly outlined the goals of the program, the goals that would be set for participating schools, and a five-year timetable for the district lead and transformation team to take over all aspects of the program (through the gradual release of responsibility from the outside experts). The plan also outlined funding needs, time commitments, and expectations for both district leaders and participating schools.

Making changes

Having reflected upon the successes and challenges of year one of implementation, Gina and the outside experts agreed that some changes would need to be made in year two of school-based implementation to ensure that participating schools were receiving the support they really needed. Two high-impact changes they proposed were rethinking the role and makeup of the district transformation team and reducing the number of schools included in the second cohort.

The DTT had worked hard in year one—that much was clear. But schools had not leveraged the DTT as effectively as Gina had hoped, which meant that something needed to change. After spending time rethinking the role and membership of the DTT, Gina determined that it would be better equipped to support schools if it were made up of instructional specialists—district-level employees (most of whom were former classroom teachers) who fully believed in the inquiry cycle and who had the added benefit of being experts in particular subject areas. Gina approached five district instructional specialists, discussed the role with them, and was happy to hear that each of them was excited about the process and fully prepared to take on the role. Reworking the DTT was a high priority for her as she planned for year two, because she realized that a DTT composed of district instructional resources would be better equipped to support participating schools. In making this change, Gina also ensured that the district was building capacity to lead the work of CSI in the future.

With this new DTT in place, Gina collaborated with the outside experts to outline in detail what the role of this team would be in supporting school transformation teams. Together, they discussed and articulated the purpose of this team.

> The purpose of the district transformation team is to build capacity at the district level to lead this work. We believe that by engaging a district transformation team on a regular basis (at all sessions and with a minimum of four direct sessions with the outside experts), they will become familiar with the process of Collaborative School Improvement, and their ability to lead this work in the future will develop. In addition, the district transformation team will be responsible for holding participating schools accountable for completing work at various stages in the process.

By clearly articulating a purpose, Gina and the outside experts had a vision for clarifying the function and commitments of the team as well. After putting the purpose, commitments, and function of the team in writing, Gina had a resource that she shared and discussed with all team members to increase their understanding of their roles.

Creating a scope for the year

With a strategic plan and a new DTT in place, Gina was ready to prepare for the second cohort of schools. Knowing that they would still need to support the cohort-one schools through their second year of implementing the inquiry cycle (as outlined in the strategic plan), Gina and the DTT sat down with the outside experts to discuss a scope and objectives for year two of school-based implementation of the inquiry cycle.

Moving forward often requires looking back; accordingly, when the first phase of planning had begun in May, Gina and the outside provider had reflected on the successes and challenges that arose during the first year of implementation with cohort-one schools. Gina felt confident that these reflections, alongside the direction outlined in the strategic plan, would help minimize challenges and encourage success. With all this information on the table, Gina and the outside provider once again met to create a scope for cohorts one and two for year two of implementation of the inquiry cycle at schools in Chandler. This scope clearly outlined dates and objectives for sessions, and specified how the DTT would support each cohort. With this detailed document in hand, Gina relaxed just a bit. She'd wrapped her brain around how it was all going to happen; now she just needed to thoughtfully select her new cohort of schools, and she'd be off and running toward year two of school-based implementation of the adopted inquiry cycle.

Selecting schools

Gina used a process for selecting cohort-two schools that was nearly identical to the one she'd used to select cohort-one schools, but there was something different in the air. Having heard the buzz around the district about the implementation of the inquiry cycle at cohort-one schools, many schools expressed interest in participating in cohort two, and each of them completed the required application in order to be considered. As Gina and the team sat down in their conference room to review each application, they worked meticulously through the process. They knew that the people doing the work affected how the work was done, and they wanted to ensure they selected schools that were prepared. The seven elementary schools that made the cut for year two were thrilled. So was Gina: she relished the prospect of having a smaller cohort of schools to work with, knowing that she could deliver more critical support to each one. Gina felt confident that this change would alleviate some of the challenges that she and the DTT had faced with providing sufficient feedback and support to the larger group of schools in cohort one.

She didn't waste any time: along with the notification that they had been chosen to participate in the second cohort, Gina provided these schools with a timeline so that they could begin reserving dates on their school calendars for sessions. In addition, Gina leveraged the expertise of the outside provider to design a training webinar that prepared the DTT members for their work: it offered an overview of the CSI project, described expectations for participating schools, and laid out the district's vision for the DTT.

YEAR THREE: IMPLEMENTING SCHOOL-BASED INQUIRY CYCLES

June 2011

To kick off a running start, Gina arranged a big meeting for the cohort-two schools. While building her agenda for this event, she spent time with the outside experts reflecting on the successes and challenges of last year's session, and made several changes to improve this session. First, she gave school teams more time to plan for their upcoming meetings. She also added individual coaching sessions to the agenda as a way to ensure that the DTT and the outside experts had the opportunity to touch base with each school team individually. As she did for each session in cohort one, Gina provided all team members from participating schools with

---

FIGURE 9.3

CHANDLER IMPLEMENTATION CALENDAR 2010–2011

JUN 2011	JUL 2011	AUG 2011	SEPT 2011	OCT 2011	NOV 2011	DEC 2011	JAN 2012	FEB 2012	MAR 2012	APR 2012	MAY 2012
STRATEGIC PLANNING											
		COHORT 2 MONTHLY TRAINING SESSIONS, COHORT 1 QUARTERLY SESSIONS									
		WEEKLY PLANNING CALLS (GINA, DTT, EDUCATION DIRECTION)									
										REFLECTED AND REFINED	

agendas, logistical information, and electronic versions of all documents prior to the session.

After all that, Gina, the DTT, and the outside experts planned the kick-off session for cohort-one schools. Their meeting would occur one day before cohort two's kick-off in June 2011, and it required all the same presession emails, agendas, and logistics. Now faced with the challenge of supporting two cohorts of schools in the implementation of the inquiry cycle, Gina and her team were experiencing what it was like to have two training sessions to prepare for—and two groups of schools to support. As parents discover with one child and a new baby, the laundry triples. However, the first child often passes useful clothing or skills to the second child. Fortunately, that happened in Gina's experience as she gained valuable information from cohort one that allowed her to enhance her support of cohort two.

Gina and the DTT designed the cohort-one session around taking stock: they gave school transformation teams the opportunity to reflect together on the successes and challenges that they had experienced throughout the first year of implementing the inquiry cycle. Then, the DTT encouraged the teams to make refinements to their work for the upcoming school year. Refining their methods was like sharpening worn but useful tools. Armed with fresh "inquiry toolboxes," school teams left the session eager to begin their next cycle. Though they predicted that new challenges would arise in year two of implementation, the STTs knew from experience that they could rely on their tools and on the DTT for support.

The following morning, a new cohort of schools sat down in the same metal chairs that their colleagues had occupied the summer before, excited about learning how to make data-driven changes that would impact both teaching and learning at their schools. Gina, Susan, the DTT, and the outside experts stood before this cohort of schools and smiled: they were prepared to partner with them in the journey and equipped to support them at every step along the way.

Because Gina and the outside experts had invested the necessary time to create a scope and calendar for year two of implementation, running two sessions in two days was both manageable and successful. Having the two cohorts convene on consecutive days provided the perfect opportunity for Gina, the new DTT, and the outside provider to reflect on each session directly after the sessions adjourned and make notes for improving future sessions.

As Gina left the second session and returned to her office, she relaxed into her chair and kicked off her shoes, shaking her head and smiling as she reflected on how far the district had come since the Data Wise Institute at Harvard. She thought about how she and a team of her colleagues had grown the idea of using inquiry to inform decision making from a one-time program for a small group of schools to a districtwide initiative. Despite all the effort and challenges, Gina took pride in the shifts that had occurred both at the district leadership level and at the school level. She could see significant changes over the past two years that had the potential to impact both the participating schools and the entire district. For instance, the district was now using data (namely, student work) to inform instruction and to drive professional development offerings. Also, district leaders were now holding schools accountable in ways that they had not in the past. She saw that alignment at all levels had increased, and that a collaborative culture was emerging in Chandler (see table 9.1).

Looking at the chart in her hands, which was created at a district leadership meeting in response to Susan and Camille gathering information on how the CSI project was going, Gina felt a sense of accomplishment. She recognized that now, more than ever before, the district was capable of engaging in and leading Collaborative School Improvement. The DTT's partnership with schools in cohorts one and two had been a success, and Gina predicted success for the future: the district's evolution via CSI would positively affect teaching and learning in Chandler for years to come.

CONCLUSION

In sharing Chandler's experiences, we hope we've accomplished two things. First, we hope that, in reading the three-year story from Chandler, you've seen that CSI requires a multiyear effort, oodles of thinking and planning, and thoughtful year-to-year adjustments. Because CSI is a set of practices—not a plug-and-play model—it is imperative that you make the practices your own, which requires thought and planning similar to the efforts in Chandler. And second, the Chandler story is chock-full of examples and tools, ripe for replication. Chandler has graciously allowed us to share them here, and we're both hopeful that its experiences can inform yours.

TABLE 9.1

CHANDLER UNIFIED SCHOOL DISTRICT, JUNE 2011

Where we've come from (partnering with schools and supporting them in improving teaching and learning)	Where we're going (partnering with schools in inquiry-based decision making)
Focus on making instructional changes based on state assessment data (which often left questions about root cause unanswered)	Focus on making instructional changes based on student work (classroom-level data)
Limited accountability for the implementation of sound instructional practices	Greater accountability for the implementation of sound instructional practices
Grade level or department team meetings as "agenda lists"	Grade level or department team meetings as professional learning communities (looking at student work)
Faculty meetings as "agenda lists" run by the principal	Faculty meetings as "data analysis" and decision making run by the school data teams
Several indiscriminate school goals, each with its own set of strategies and action steps	One school goal with aligned strategies and action steps
Minimal collaborative conversations among principals about instructional practices and teacher observation processes	Collaborative conversations among principals about instructional practices and teacher observation processes
Unsuccessfully using benchmark assessment data to determine student performance	Successfully implementing sound formative assessment processes (indicators of student performance)

Source: Chandler Unified School District, Chandler, Arizona

EXHIBIT 9.1

SCOPE FOR CHANDLER UNIFIED SCHOOL DISTRICT 2010–2011

Session # / Month	Data Wise (DW) Chapter	School Transformation Team Objectives
1 / June	1–8 Focus on 1 and 3	■ Understand program objectives and the role of the school transformation team program. ■ Understand and apply key principles imbedded in DW Chapters 1 and 3. ■ Appreciate strengths of team members. ■ Understand and practice components of effective group work and group meetings. ■ Develop team fears, hopes, and norms. ■ Analyze school data and choose "educational question" to frame data overview meeting. ■ Create plan for data overview meeting.
2 / August	3–4	■ Understand and apply key principles imbedded in DW Chapters 3–4. ■ Develop plan to dig into data.
3 / September	1, 4–5	■ Revisit norms and progress in collaborative work. ■ Understand and apply key principles imbedded in DW Chapters 4–5. ■ Practice classroom observation as a potential "examining instruction" technique. (p. 103). ■ Develop an examining instruction plan (DW p. 106, 111).
4 / October	5–6	■ Understand and apply key principles imbedded in DW Chapters 5–6. ■ Create wire-framed action plan. ■ Develop plan to engage staff in creating key components of action plan.
5 / November	6–7	■ Understand and apply key principles imbedded in DW Chapters 6–7. ■ Develop initial plan to assess progress, including short-, medium-, and long-term data.
6 / January	7–8	■ Understand and apply key principles imbedded in DW Chapters 7–8. ■ Take stock of current progress both in terms of student learning and in terms of implementation of action plan. ■ Develop key next steps to properly "act and assess."
7 / February	8	■ Act and assess.
8 / March	8	■ Act and assess.
9 / April	8	■ Act and assess.
10 / May	3–4	■ Create a data overview. ■ Dig into student data.

Source: Chandler Unified School District, Chandler, Arizona

EXHIBIT 9.2

YEARLONG TIMELINE TEMPLATE

June/July

June 14th: Full day data team session	*Tasks:* ■ Analyze AIMS data (collect additional data if needed) ■ Finalize your educational question (to inform planning for data overview meeting) ■ Create a Data Overview ■ Submit DO slides for review (by July 8th) and receive feedback (by July 20th) ■ Reserve date for whole-school Data Overview meeting

August

Present Data Overview to entire staff prior to August 15th August 16th: Full day data team session	*Tasks:* ■ Come up with focus questions (to inform "digging into data") ■ Collect student work for looking at student work (LASW) protocol ■ Engage staff in LASW protocol ■ Define a learner-centered problem (LCP) with staff ■ Submit LCP for review by September 9th

September

September 13th: Full day data team session Engage staff in protocol to select a problem of practice (PoP) prior to October 12th	*Tasks:* ■ Examine instruction (observations or survey) ■ Submit PoP for review by October 12th ■ Collect research-based instructional strategies that you may implement to address the PoP you identified

October

October 18th: Full day data team session Present and model instructional strategies to staff and determine implementation indicators prior to November 14th	*Tasks:* ■ Select 2–3 instructional strategies to present to staff ■ Submit selected instructional strategy and implementation indicators for review by November 14th ■ Create an assessment inventory and select short- and medium-term assessments to monitor progress in focus area ■ Create a Plan to Assess Progress (PtAP) and enter baseline scores and goals for short-, medium-, and long-term assessments ■ Create wire-framed Action Plan and submit for review prior to November 14th ■ Implement instructional strategy (collect baseline data prior to the implementation of your selected strategy)

(continued on next page)

November

November 29th: Full day data team session	*Tasks:* ■ Continue implementing selected instructional strategy ■ Collect short-term data ■ Finalize Action Plan and Plan to Assess Progress by December 9th for review

December

	Tasks: ■ Continue implementing selected instructional strategy ■ Collect short-term data ■ Finalize Action Plan and Plan to Assess Progress and submit for review by December 9th

January

January 24th: Full day data team session	*Tasks:* ■ Create a plan to engage entire staff in observing practice protocol ■ Submit plan for engaging staff in observing practice protocol by February 3rd ■ Collect short- and medium-term data ■ Create and display medium-term data chart

February/March

February 28th: Full day data team session Engage entire staff in observing practice protocol prior to March 30th	*Tasks:* ■ Collect short-term data ■ Write observation reflection and submit prior to April 2nd

April

April 4th: Full day data team session Engage in medium-term data analysis with whole school prior to May 4th	*Tasks:* ■ Collect medium-term data and add to data chart ■ Display data chart in school where all teachers/staff can see it ■ Submit medium-term data chart for review prior to May 4th ■ Create a 5-minute PowerPoint presentation to tell your story at next data team session

May

May 16th: Full day data team session Share your "story" with staff and engage staff in activity to gauge ownership prior to June 11th	*Task:* ■ Begin collecting data for End of Cycle (EoC) Data Summary (student work, teacher interviews, student interviews, assessment data, etc.)

June/July

June 13th: Full day data team session	*Task:* ■ Create End of Cycle Data Summary ■ Reserve time to present EoC Data Summary to entire staff in August

Source: Chandler Unified School District, Chandler, Arizona

EXHIBIT 9.3

EXECUTIVE SUMMARY

The Chandler Unified School District seeks to engage all schools in the district in the CSI project over the course of five years (2010–2015). Schools that participate in the CSI project will receive intensive training and coaching on *Data Wise: A Step-by-Step Guide to Using Assessment Results to Improve Teaching and Learning* (Harvard Education Press, 2005). The district has hired Dr. Trent Kaufman (President, Education Direction), chapter author of *Data Wise in Action* (Harvard Education Press, 2007), to help lead this work. The goal of the project is to aid participating schools in developing collaborative cultures of data-informed decision making, **focusing intently on classroom instruction as the greatest lever for school improvement.**

CSI is a process, a way that districts and schools committed to continuous improvement operate. It is a structure upon which many schools and districts around the country rely to collaboratively define learner-centered problems and problems of practice, address those problems with targeted instructional interventions, and regularly measure progress against collaboratively identified goals. Participation in the program is not traditional professional development; participating schools will learn and practice protocols to engage their staff in a schoolwide inquiry and improvement process. School teams will be coached to make this process their own, making school-level decisions about schoolwide efforts to dramatically improve teaching and learning in their building.

We believe that, by engaging all schools within the district in the CSI project, the impact on teaching practices and student learning will be significant and that, districtwide, a culture of inquiry will emerge. This culture of success (built upon data-driven decision making) will become a driving force that will lead our district toward achieving our goals for academic excellence as outlined in Journey 2020.

STRATEGIC PLANNING METHODOLOGY

What we will do:

- Create a school improvement plan (document) that schools could add to as they move through the process
    1. Clearly define plan for improving teaching and learning
    2. Highlight the ultimate goal of the this program—increases in student learning
    3. Include a plan to assess progress

- Clearly define the role of the district transformation team
    1. Learn the data-driven inquiry cycle (*Data Wise*)
    2. Embed accountability measures (review plans, provide feedback)
- Support schools
    1. Build capacity to lead this work

Ultimate goal of the program: Increases in student learning

- All schools must set goals for each year. Over time, these goals will align with the academic goals for Journey 2020—to exceed state AIMS scores at all grade levels in math and reading, to score in the top 25% of Arizona districts at all AIMS grade levels in reading and math, and to increase the percent of 3rd grade students reading at grade level.
- The district data team will provide a "menu" of goals to the teams. Each school will be required to select one of the following goals for the year:
    1. 10% growth in student proficiency in identified strand of focus, 5% growth in student proficiency in identified subject area of focus
    2. Cutting the achievement gap in half (for underserved students)

School Improvement Plan Process

- Establish a plan to "build in" the support for schools beyond their second year.
- District data team members will be responsible for reviewing these plans and providing ongoing feedback to schools.
- Schools will be encouraged to fill in their plans along the way (action plan, goals, plans to assess progress), and to revise/add to these plans as needed. This should not be viewed as a static document. We encourage the district to introduce it as an ongoing effort to document improvement at the school level.

How can we ensure the CSI Project is a schoolwide effort?

- District leadership, with help from the district data team, will create a plan to address this issue.
    1. The application process requires school leadership to present the CSI Project to the entire school staff.
    2. A school-based transformation team, which includes school leadership, is established to complete the application process.

3. The school-based transformation team participates in extensive professional development to create a school improvement plan.

4. The school leader may choose to require the school-based team to lead in the creation and revision of the school improvement plan (with input from the entire staff).

5. Because of the nature of the Data Wise Inquiry cycle, teams could easily engage their teachers/staff in helping to make decisions along the way as they create this plan.

Clearly defined School Improvement Plan focused on teaching and learning

- Action Plan: Much like the "action plans" that teams created in cohort 1, this portion of the plan will clearly define the following:

  1. The identified learner-centered problem
  2. The defined problem of practice
  3. The instructional strategy(s) that schools have chosen to implement
  4. The school's plan to implement the strategy(s) with fidelity across the board (through the creation of implementation indicators)

- Plan to Assess Progress: As part of the school improvement plan, all schools must submit a plan to assess progress in student learning. This plan will include the following:

  1. Plans for collecting short-, medium-, and long-term data

     a. Names of assessment tools, plans for collecting, scoring, and analyzing the data
     b. Short-term data
        i. Collected by individual teachers on a monthly basis (at minimum)
     c. Medium-term data
        ii. Collected by teams (grade, department, or transformation team) no fewer than three times over the course of the year (in addition to the collection of baseline data at the beginning of the school year)
     d. Long-term data
        iii. Collected by teams annually and disaggregated to show growth in the identified areas

  2. Goals for student growth at each interval

     a. Ambitious and achievable goals to be determined for each assessment

Source: Chandler Unified School District, Chandler, Arizona

A Litmus Test for CSI

I didn't fail the test; I just found 100 ways to do it wrong.
—*Benjamin Franklin*

The test of the artist does not lie in the will with which he goes to work, but in the excellence of the work he produces.
—*Thomas Aquinas*

Test fast, fail fast, adjust fast. —*Tom Peters*

Litmus is a handy scientific tool. Technically, *litmus* is a mix of various dyes used on thin paper to determine acidity, but the word has morphed across multiple disciplines and applications to mean "a set of criteria that demonstrate acceptability." *Litmus tests* in politics are candidate-potential barometers; in human resources departments, they are nonnegotiable interviewee characteristics.

As authors, we are tempted by the concept of litmus. Why? Because sometimes you just want to know where things stand—especially when you're knee-deep in a complicated process like Collaborative School Improvement. In this conclusion, we want to provide a litmus-test-type tool—a set of questions—that will indicate how effectively districts are implementing CSI.

We realize we are playing in murky territory—that a litmus test for CSI is problematic for a variety of reasons. For one, success with CSI (as we've likely overemphasized in the pages of this book) should start and end with increases in student learning. And those increases in student learning will have come from improvements in teaching. Since *doing CSI well* is most certainly *not* the end goal, measuring it might lead to overemphasizing it. Additionally, CSI is a set of practices that are nuanced—mastered over many years and iterations. At some level, then, boiling CSI down to a litmus test demeans the model.

Nevertheless, the benefit of some measurement is too great; we feel compelled to offer a concrete tool of measurement, even acknowledging the flaws of doing so. Therefore, we will qualify the litmus test that follows not as the ultimate indicator of success, but merely a gauge of whether you have grasped and applied the fundamental concepts of CSI. We also don't claim that this litmus test is exhaustive: doing so would oversimplify the large changes you are making to the way your district does business. Therefore, our test's probing questions address the degree to which you have become a *partner* in school improvement. We will leave the ultimate test of whether your work has been effective to the measurements that reveal whether your students are learning more, and to the practices that indicate whether teaching is improving in your district.

In short, then, the upcoming questions compose our litmus test for the following:

- Whether you have grasped and applied the fundamental concepts of CSI
- The degree to which you have become a partner to schools in their improvement efforts

LITMUS TEST FOR COLLABORATIVE SCHOOL IMPROVEMENT

1. What do you know about the improvement work of the schools in your district?
   a. Do you know the root causes that each school is addressing?
   b. Do you know the instructional strategies and overarching action plan each school has created to address those root causes?
   c. Are you aware of the performance goals the schools have set for medium- and long-term assessments?
   d. Do you know whether the medium-term measures are indicating success?
   e. Do you know whether midcourse adjustments have been made to any of your schools' action plans based on that medium-term data?

This first set of questions gauges intimacy between schools and their district. We have yet to see true partnerships happen between schools and districts when district transformation team members stayed an arm's length from the nitty-gritty details of school plans. We know that it can be difficult and tedious to keep track of multiple schools and their diverse plans. However, the key is to know enough to provide helpful feedback, to connect various schools with others working on similar issues, and to be able to report to your board about the success of the program by school and across the aggregate set of schools.

The risk in tracking closely is that schools may begin to treat these plans as compliance activities. School plans should be created by and for school teams. You don't want schools to create plans with the district as their intended audience. A scenario where your schools don't reference their plans is the antithesis of what CSI can accomplish. However, the simple act of collecting the details of your schools' plans can backfire by sending a signal to schools that they are somehow making the plans and collecting the measurements *for you*! The key is for districts to use the information to *help* the schools, supporting their ownership.

2. Consider the elements of question one where you felt confident answering "yes, we know," and mentally describe what role you played in helping schools develop those elements of their improvement work.

Knowing the intricate details of your schools' improvement work will help you play a partner role, but it is not a fail-safe indicator that you are actually playing that role. We have seen many amazing spreadsheets on the minutiae of school improvement plans. Some of those spreadsheets are kept by district leaders who are also intimately involved in helping schools create and execute those plans. Others are kept by district leaders who are entirely uninvolved.

This speaks to the balancing act we described in our response to question one. Keeping track of your schools is necessary but not sufficient to becoming a true partner with them. We know this is difficult and have seen it take some time for DTT members to strike the right balance. That's OK—the point is that you are making the effort to track what your schools are working on and how it's going, and simultaneously participating as a partner in helping them create and execute their plans.

Now, consider any parts of question one where you answered "no." We encourage you to pick one of those areas and commit to getting that information tomorrow (or this afternoon). This next step will help you increase your awareness of your schools' work, and will better equip you to dig in and help them with it.

3. How much time did you spend yesterday (or on a typical day) supporting your schools' improvement work?

District leaders who have grasped CSI spend the majority of the day in support of schools' efforts to improve teaching and learning. Time spent discussing or implementing plans that do not directly support schools' needs is considered less important in the CSI model.

Obviously, district leaders have functional responsibilities to maintain, such as pupil support and human resources, but even those can be refocused to support schools' plans. Consider a DTT member who is the district's HR director. Through his DTT work, he has learned firsthand that many schools are addressing the racial achievement gap. He is much better equipped to create hiring processes that support that priority need. For example, he could add further candidate scoring criteria to potential teacher or administrator hires, allocating extra "points" to those who have narrowed racial achievement gaps in their prior schools.

District leaders who are actively engaged with schools and their improvement are invited by school team members to their buildings to participate in staff meetings. Such district leaders provide feedback to STTs about their team functioning and observe instruction as part of the team's monitoring of their school's action plan. Hopefully that's how you want to spend your day. District leaders who are true partners are available to help school leaders build agendas and make plans for STT meetings. Additionally, engaged DTT members frequently connect individual STT members with those from other CSI schools to effectively leverage the tools and resources each is creating.

Now, getting invited to school buildings is a sure sign that you have become a true partner, but getting there starts with baby steps. We haven't seen this happen in year one of CSI—it gets more common as schools realize that the district is going to stick with CSI, and as the DTT builds the internal capacity for the work. In the short run, we encourage you to pick one way you can increase your support of schools' improvement efforts. One district leader with whom we work ends each day with a simple rhetorical question: "What did I do today to improve the learning of the students in my district?" This reflective thought process has created space for her to help schools in ways she previously thought were outside the purview of her formal position.

4. What were the major topics and action items from your most recent district transformation team meeting?

a. First of all, are you having regular district transformation meetings?

Hopefully, yes. The topics of discussion at these meetings can be strong indicators of your focus on CSI. The two overarching purposes of the DTT are to engage directly in inquiry (in similar fashion to the schools) and to handle the planning required for CSI. Topics that align with these purposes might include analyzing data and creating action plans (aligned with the first purpose) and collaborating with the outside providers on the content of an upcoming training session (aligned with the latter purpose).

b. To what extent have you embraced team norms?

In addition to *what* topics you discuss, *how* you discuss them may be a strong indicator of your grasp of CSI. To enhance your use of team norms, at the conclusion of an upcoming DTT meeting, try having each team member cite evidence for one norm that your team has followed and one norm that it hasn't. Then share the results of that discussion with STT members as you discuss their work with them. Embracing norms—and then modeling the vulnerability required to actually change meeting patterns in your district—will propel your leadership, not diminish it.

c. How well does your DTT make use of effective team meeting tools such as protocols, agendas, and time keepers?

If your meetings result in action, that's a good sign that you are exemplifying the work of effective transformation teams. For more detail, examine the items on a recent agenda and note whether the collaborative discussions and tasks were best done as a whole group. If each meeting item is thoughtfully assigned either to the whole group or to individuals or subgroups—depending on the nature of the item—that's another sign that your DTT has effectively grasped the basic principles of teaming for CSI.

5. When was the last time you have taken something off your schools' and teachers' plates?

Admittedly, this is a hard one. Your first job is to convince yourself that doing more is actually about doing less! Remember: high-priority needs. Root causes. Narrow entry points. Aligning resources. By focusing on these key things, you will get more boats in your harbor to rise—not by addressing each and every boat. Go back and read chapter 4. No, really, go back and read it (speed-read if you have to). For the sales job you will need to do in your district, you have to really believe this important point.

Once you are convinced, it is time to convince others. We've given you some tools for doing that in chapter 4, but remember to help your team understand that the recent history of U.S. public education proves our point. Most districts have tried multiple initiatives aimed at myriad student groups and curricular areas with minimal or no success. Trying to address all the problems in your district at once is tantamount to boiling the ocean. You can try, but you won't even heat it up!

6. If I ask a principal in your district to tell me what the district's role is in school improvement, what would she say?

"I don't know"—an answer we hear all too often in schools across the country—is not the right response from a CSI school. STT members, including principals, should have a clear sense of the district's role. "Partner" should be the picture they paint as they consider your role in their school improvement efforts.

Having said that, we know you likely have large hurdles to overcome to become a true partner. If it took thirty or more years to develop the current culture of your district—where district leaders are perhaps seen more as the enemy than as trusted teammates—it is understandable that the new culture you are trying to create won't take hold right away.

We hope at this point your burning question is something like this: "How does a district transformation team member earn the role of partner in the minds of school staff members? How can I begin today?" That's the whole purpose of this book. Practicing what's preached in this book will get you most of the way there. In other words, embracing the practices contained herein—and doing so repeatedly and consistently over time—will do wonders for your relationships with and influence in the schools you serve.

We hope that this litmus test—such as it is—has both given you cause to celebrate and provided motivation for your next steps. We encourage you to notice what you're doing well, and keep doing it. Do it more often. We also invite you to look honestly at the things you can improve without feeling overwhelmed. Having room to grow line upon line is enough reason to return to work each day. You'll see improvements over time as you continue. Please revisit this litmus test through the months and years of your efforts in CSI—we predict you'll come away with new insights each time.

Your students *can* achieve more through improved classroom instruction. Schools will sense your desire to truly help them help their children. And you *can* more strongly influence classroom instruction through your role as a partner to schools in their improvement efforts. Just like Sherlock needed Dr. Watson, your schools need you. And, like Sherlock, your schools won't always admit that need, but they'll be grateful when the results begin to appear. Keep at it. You'll get there.

> Alone we can do so little; together we can do so much.
>
> —*Helen Keller*

CSI as a Tool for Systemic Change

The practices embedded in Collaborative School Improvement have the capacity to create and sustain large-scale improvements in teaching and student learning within and across schools in your district. As we have worked alongside districts engaged in widescale reform, we have witnessed firsthand the obstacles to improving teaching and learning at scale that have been illustrated through decades of education research. The practices of CSI work precisely to address the impediments common to many of these unsuccessful improvement efforts. In doing so, CSI holds promise for creating meaningful changes in teaching and learning across schools by:

- Maintaining a focus on the core of teaching and learning over the structures of schooling
- Responding to the local context, including school-, teacher-, and student-specific needs
- Acknowledging the school culture and the cultural changes necessary to impact teaching and student learning
- Integrating sustained and relevant professional development

Research demonstrates that a failure to address each of the aforementioned factors has been both common and debilitating to past improvement efforts. Only through understanding these factors are we sufficiently equipped to address them in future improvement efforts, and namely in CSI. Rather than maintaining a focus on school structures, we can invest our resources in the heart of teaching and learning in the classroom. These efforts must be context specific, providing for ongoing and relevant professional development that acknowledges the local expertise as well as drives changes in the culture of teaching and learning. Past decades tell us this is no easy task. Yet, by engaging in the practices of Collaborative School Improvement, school and district leaders can build a partnership that challenges these common pitfalls of school improvement efforts. Through CSI, the potential for change—identified and implemented at the local level—is realized.

A FOCUS ON THE CORE OF TEACHING AND LEARNING

To their detriment, school improvement efforts commonly focus on improving the structures of school rather than directly impacting the school's core: teaching and learning.[1] Even a quick look at school improvement plans makes this point apparent. More often than not, improvement efforts tackle scheduling, curricular resources, and opportunities for extended learning more frequently than they tackle the deeper practices of classroom instruction. This shortcoming is illustrated in David Tyack's infamous metaphor comparing reform efforts with meteors—they attract a lot of attention, but deposit very little of anything in the classroom.[2]

The simple reality is that the classroom has been largely impervious to reform. Despite efforts to improve education, changes are not happening at the level where they matter the most—in the classroom. As any teacher or administrator can attest, maintaining a focus on improving instruction is hard work, requiring significant training and enormous effort. Alternatively, improving the noninstructional aspects of school is fairly straightforward work, directing attention to these significantly simpler endeavors. The complexities of instruction, particularly when placed in the context of the instructional core, make improving teaching and learning an ambitious (although possible!) objective. As one researcher quipped, "The sad fact is that most reforms don't acknowledge the realities of classroom teaching, where both God and the devil are in the details."[3]

And while some of the structural reforms of recent decades have been implemented with intentions to trickle down to the classroom, the gap between school structures and classroom practice is too large to hope that structural reforms will make an instructional difference in classroom. As David Gordon notes, "Too often reforms have focused on big-picture issues—school governance, organization, curriculum, accountability, and so forth—without taking into account how decisions affect what happens on the front lines, where improvement is most needed."[4] Experience tells us that changes in the ways schools are structured have failed to produce the higher student achievement desired. In other words, reforms must focus on how implemented changes will be embodied in classroom instruction—the front lines of education reform. Efforts to improve student performance will continue to fail as long as they neglect to impact the heart of teaching and learning: the relationship between teachers, student, and content.

Collaborative School Improvement holds promise for school improvement efforts through providing districts, and the schools within them, a structure for using data to directly inform teaching and student learning. The inquiry cycle focuses attention on what matters most: student learning and its relationship to instructional practice. Through the practices of CSI—including adopting an inquiry cycle and narrowing the focus—teachers and school leaders are equipped to understand the root causes of learning problems and thus, to address them with relevant and intentional instructional adjustments. The structure that the adopted inquiry cycle provides is just the first step. Only through the hard work of teachers, school leaders, and district leaders, and their diligent focus on classroom instruction, will inquiry translate into improved student outcomes.

While the practices of CSI contribute to the development of a partnership between the district and the schools they serve, the purpose of this partnership is to leverage resources toward instructional improvements. The case study districts we follow throughout this book illustrate the ways in which district-school partnerships can facilitate a refinement of instruction that better meets students' needs, resulting in improved student outcomes. For example, engagement in CSI in Portland led the district to not only create resources for improving writing instruction, but also to support schools in the implementation of those resources in the classroom—support that promoted writing instruction districtwide.

ATTENTION TO THE LOCAL CONTEXT

Any educator can attest to the unique environment that exists within a school community, one that is influenced by students, parents, and educators, who themselves bring a diversity of experiences and perspectives. Unfortunately, many reforms have ignored this important element. Reforms too often come from external sources, which lack a thorough understanding of the specific learning community.[5] These externally created, one-size-fits-all reforms neglect to account for local context and thus are insufficient to ensure effective implementation in a specific setting. This is particularly problematic for the implementation of instructional improvements, because effective teaching "requires flexibility, a wide repertoire of strategies, and use of judgment in complex, non-routine situations where multiple goals are being pursued."[6] Simultaneously, external reforms ignore the local expertise within a school community, failing to harness the power of cooperation among teams of professionals.[7] After all, unless reform efforts leverage the internal expertise in classrooms, how can we expect them to meet the needs of a variety of complex classroom contexts? This neglect is akin to prescribing treatment for a patient based on a single symptom. Without a deeper understanding of the patient's medical history and lifestyle—gleaned from the patient's primary care physician and the patient himself—the treatment is likely to miss the mark.

The shortcomings of reforms that neglect the local context should not be interpreted as a call to remove policy makers and administrators from reform efforts. These individuals are critical to maintaining the big-picture view that complements the perspective and expertise of those embedded in a local context. Not surprisingly, recent evidence suggests that a dynamic approach involving policy makers, district- and school-level administrators, as well as classroom teachers may yield the most fruitful results.[8] Simply put, for reform efforts to be most effective, it's essential to involve all players, rather than relying solely on the team captain to win the game.

CSI calls for the implementation of a data-driven inquiry cycle, which by its very nature depends on the expertise of a variety of stakeholders, including teachers and school leaders. While grounded in research-based practices of collective data-driven decision making, CSI requires the local contributions and perspectives of teachers to use the cycle to inform classroom-level decisions. Rather than a top-down approach to school improvement, CSI provides schools with a process for a whole faculty to identify school-specific needs, their root causes, and relevant instructional solutions. While the steps of the inquiry cycle itself will remain consistent across schools, the identified focus of each school—from the priority needs to the relevant instructional solutions—will vary in response to the context.

The results of CSI are evident throughout the case study districts we highlight in this book. In Evansville, STTs involved their entire faculties in decision making throughout the Data Wise Improvement Process.[9] The transformation team at each school in the district engaged its faculty in examining data to identify a school-wide need, explore its root causes, and implement a relevant instructional strategy. Rather than a top-down approach that dictated instructional improvements, teachers used their varied perspectives and expertise to collectively identify and implement changes in their practice.

While the guiding objective (improvements in student learning) and the process (the Data Wise Improvement Process) are consistent across schools in Evansville, each building has approached the work in a manner that reflects the specific needs of its students and teachers. For example, North High School identified students' difficulties with reading comprehension and recognized a need for teachers to better support students' understanding of directional vocabulary. Across the district, Central High identified students' weakness analyzing information and applying critical thinking skills. Following further exploration of this need, Central teachers engaged in conversations on best practices around critical thinking and implementation of those practices. While both schools have received similar support from the district, each school has engaged its faculty to identify and address context-specific needs, a practice that utilized local expertise to drive improvements in teaching and learning.

ATTENTION TO THE SCHOOL CULTURE

Neglecting to focus on changing the culture of schools—including the internal accountability and working relationships that exist among faculty members—has further impeded school improvement efforts.[10] Changing culture—whether in a school or any other setting—presents a challenge, yet culture change is necessary if teaching and learning are to be truly impacted.[11] If reforms fail to acknowledge the existing culture—and the way current beliefs and behaviors hinder improvement—new practices will fail to embed themselves in the existing environment.

Not unlike reforms that fail to focus on classroom instruction, reforms that fail to impact school culture have limited potential to create real, permanent change. In fact, most initiatives have little or no lasting impact on a school because they do not make a dent in the culture of the school or of teaching.[12] Even reforms created to change the way in which teachers engage with one another and approach improvement—such as professional learning communities—often result in only superficial changes. For example, teachers may have a new structure for collaboration, only to engage in the same conversations that have dominated shared professional time.

As demonstrated through the practices of CSI, culture change is a necessary element of creating meaningful impact in classrooms. CSI proposes a structure for school improvement—an inquiry cycle—alongside the development of skills that cultivate effective collaboration and teaming. CSI recognizes that only through the acknowledgment of the need for changes in school culture—including the way in which colleagues engage in conversations about teaching and student learning—will improvement occur in classrooms across a district.

As illustrated throughout this book, the case study districts engaged in new ways of teaming and collaborating, changes that often pushed up against established patterns of dialogue. In Chandler, each school engaged in peer observations, where teachers entered one another's classrooms to collect data that provided starting points for impactful conversations on teaching and student learning. This practice deconstructed the established silos in which classrooms in most districts exist, perhaps one of the most consistent cultural elements of the teaching profession, and provided a context for these conversations.

SUSTAINED AND RELEVANT PROFESSIONAL DEVELOPMENT

Effective school improvement also demands a shift in the way that teachers are expected to engage in professional development (PD). The established norm of one-shot PD sessions—all too frequently handed down by experts and detached from a teacher's classroom context, and in which more than 90 percent of U.S. teachers participate—further inhibits effective school improvement.[13] Instead, reform efforts must engage teachers in sustained collaborative PD that provides opportunities for application of and reflection on instructional practice—in other words, job-embedded PD. Instructional improvements result from PD where teachers

> follow a cycle of continuous improvement that begins with examining student data to determine the areas of greatest student need, pinpointing areas where additional educator learning is necessary, identifying and creating learning experiences to address these adult needs, developing powerful lessons and assessments, applying new strategies in the classroom, refining new learning into more powerful lessons and assessments, reflecting on the impact on student learning, and repeating the cycle with new goals.[14]

These practices will sound remarkably familiar if you have recently read the chapters of this book.

As noted in the efforts of all three case study districts, professional development within CSI is embedded in the ongoing implementation of the inquiry cycle. The work of inquiry, by its very nature, is embedded in the daily practice of teachers. Through the practices of CSI, teachers, school, and district leaders engage with one another in conversations about student needs and relevant instructional solutions. Furthermore, when the district partners with schools in this work, they are equipped to provide focused PD that responds to the schools' needs.

WIDESCALE SCHOOL IMPROVEMENT

As summarized here (and documented in a steady stream of education literature), the challenges to effective school improvement persist. Yet, we also have clarity as to how we can create more effective school improvement efforts that focus on what matters most—teaching and learning—and engage teachers, school leaders, and district leaders in a process that fundamentally changes the culture of schools.

What it takes is an undeniable focus on changing what occurs in the classroom each day. Inquiry equips teachers and school and district leaders with a process for examining the very heart of education: the classroom, and more specifically, the interaction among students, teachers, and content (the instructional core). Collaborative School Improvement clarifies the practices in which districts and schools can engage to leverage each other's expertise and perspective. In implementing these practices, they are able to create meaningful changes in teaching and learning districtwide—thereby holding promise for the students and communities you serve in your daily practice.

Introduction

1. Arthur Conan Doyle, "The Adventure of the Creeping Man," in *The Complete Sherlock Holmes, Volume II* (New York: Barnes and Noble Classics, 2003), 601.

2. Arthur Conan Doyle, *The Hound of the Baskervilles* (London: George Newnes, 1902), 2–3.

3. United States Department of Education, "Highlights from PISA 2009: Performance of U.S. 15-Year-Old Students in Reading, Mathematics, and Science Literacy in an International Context" (Washington, DC: National Center for Education Statistics, 2010), iii–iv.

4. Michael Fullan, *The Moral Imperative Realized* (Thousand Oaks, CA: Corwin Press, 2010), 39.

5. Meredith I. Honig et al., "Central Office Transformation for District-wide Teaching and Learning Improvement," (Seattle: Center for the Study of Teaching and Policy, April 2010), 1–4.

6. Richard DuFour and Robert J. Marzano, *Leaders of Learning: How District, School, and Classroom Leaders Improve Student Achievement* (Bloomington, IN: Solution Tree Press, 2011), 19–20, 45.

7. *Inquiry cycles* are formal processes that many organizations follow to investigate and uncover problems, create plans for addressing them, and measure progress toward alleviating them. If you are unfamiliar with the term *inquiry cycles*, reading chapter 1 first will help clarify the framework described in the introduction.

8. United States Department of Education, "Use of Education Data at the Local Level: From Accountability to Instructional Improvement" (Washington, DC, 2010), 26–38; Linda Darling-Hammond and Nikole Richardson, "Teacher Learning: What Matters?", *Educational Leadership* 66, no. 5 (2009), 46–53; Victoria L. Bernhardt, *Data, Data Everywhere: Bringing All the Data Together for Continuous School Improvement* (Larchmont, NY: Eye on Education, 2009), 1–6.

9. United States Department of Education, "Use of Education," xii.

10. We developed the term *Collaborative School Improvement*, which we use to reference our work throughout this book, for the purposes of sharing our thinking. While the case study districts are engaged in the process we've described throughout the book, they use various terms for the work.

11. Interview with Gina Vukovich, Chandler Unified School District, August 23, 2011; Indiana Department of Education, "Find School and Corporation Data Reports," http://www.doe.in.gov/data/reports.html; Portland Public Schools, "Facts and figures 2010–11," http://www.pps.k12.or.us/files/cipa/PPS-InfoSheet-2010-11-V06.pdf.

12. The CUSD participants attended the Data Wise Summer Institute at the Harvard Graduate School of Education (HGSE). For more information on HGSE's Programs in Professional Education, visit http://www.gse.harvard.edu/ppe.

13. Kathryn Parker Boudett, Elizabeth A. City, and Richard J. Murnane, eds., *Data Wise: A Step-by-Step Guide to Using Assessment Results to Improve Teaching and Learning* (Cambridge, MA: Harvard Education Press, 2005).

14. Throughout this book, we refer to *Data Wise* as a book (see previous endnote). We use the phrase *Data Wise Improvement Process* when referring to the steps explained in the book.

Chapter 1

1. Douglas B. Reeves, "Saving Money and Time for School Systems," webinar for The Leadership and Learning Center, June 27, 2011, http://www.leadandlearn.com/multimedia-resource-center/webinars/saving-money-and-time-school-systems.

2. Linda Darling-Hammond et al., "Professional Learning in the Learning Profession: A Status Report on Teacher Development in the U.S. and Abroad" (Dallas: National Staff Development Council, 2009), 3.

3. Douglas B. Reeves, "Pull the Weeds Before You Plant the Flowers," *Educational Leadership* 64, no. 1 (2006): 89–90.

4. Linda Darling-Hammond and Nikole Richardson, "Teacher Learning: What Matters?", *Educational Leadership* 66, no. 5 (2009), 46–53; Nancy Love, ed., *Using Data to Improve Learning for All: A Collaborative Inquiry Approach* (Thousand Oaks, CA: Corwin Press, 2009), 97–161. Victoria L. Bernhardt, *Data Analysis for Continuous School Improvement*, 2nd ed. (Larchmont, NY: Eye on Education, 2004), 3.

5. Margaret Goertz, Leslie Nabors Oláh, and Matthew Riggan, "From Testing to Teaching: The Use of Interim Assessments in Classroom Instruction" (Philadelphia: Consortium for Policy Research in Education, 2010), 8.

6. Kathryn Parker Boudett, Elizabeth A. City, and Richard J. Murnane, eds., *Data Wise: A Step-by-Step Guide to Using Assessment Results to Improve Teaching and Learning* (Cambridge, MA: Harvard Education Press, 2005).

7. Elizabeth A. City et al., *Instructional Rounds in Education: A Network Approach to Improving Teaching and Learning* (Cambridge, MA: Harvard Education Press, 2009), 21. We will simply refer to this concept as the *instructional core* hereafter without additional citations.

8. Deborah Loewenberg Ball and David K. Cohen, "Developing Practice, Developing Practitioners," in *Teaching as the Learning Profession: Handbook of Policy and Practice*, eds. Linda Darling-Hammond and Gary Sykes (San Francisco, CA: Jossey-Bass, 1999), 3–32. Richard Elmore has discussed the instructional core in multiple publications, including *Instructional Rounds in Education*, authored with City, Fiarman, and Teitel.

9. Chip Heath and Dan Heath, *Switch: How to Change Things When Change Is Hard* (New York: Broadway, 2010), 27–32.

10. United States Department of Education, "Implementing Data-Informed Decision Making in Schools—Teacher Access, Supports and Use" (Washington, DC, 2009), 47.

11. Please refer to www.lasw.org for a substantive introduction to this topic.

12. Joseph P. McDonald et al., *The Power of Protocols: An Educator's Guide to Better Practice* (New York: Teachers College Press, 2007), 7.

13. Boudett, City, and Murnane, *Data Wise*, 138.

Chapter 2

1. Richard DuFour and Robert J. Marzano, *Leaders of Learning: How District, School, and Classroom Leaders Improve Student Achievement* (Bloomington, IN: Solution Tree Press, 2011), 33.

2. Kathryn Parker Boudett, Elizabeth A. City, and Richard J. Murnane, eds., *Data Wise: A Step-by-Step Guide to Using Assessment Results to Improve Teaching and Learning* (Cambridge, MA: Harvard Education Press, 2005), 11–55.

3. Fred Newmann et al., "Instructional Program Coherence: What It Is and Why It Should Guide School Improvement Policy," *Education Evaluation and Policy Analysis* 23, no. 4 (2011): 298.

Chapter 3

1. David T. Conley and Paul Goldman, "Facilitative Leadership: How Principals Lead without Dominating," *Oregon School Study Council Bulletin* 37, no. 9 (1994), 4.

2. Diane Dunlap and Paul Goldman, "Power as a 'System of Authority' vs. Power as a 'System of Facilitation,'" (paper presented at the annual meeting of the American Educational Research Association, Boston, Massachusetts, April 16–20, 1990), 20–21.

3. If you are not familiar with the word *protocols* used in this way, please refer to two of our favorite resources on this topic. First, you can find solid rationale for, and examples of the use of, protocols in Joseph P. McDonald et al., *The Power of Protocols: An Educator's Guide to Better Practice* (New York: Teachers College Press, 2003). Additionally, you can find a plethora of examples of protocols from the National School Reform Faculty at www.nsrfharmony.org.

4. Richard DuFour and Robert J. Marzano, *Leaders of Learning: How District, School, and Classroom Leaders Improve Student Achievement* (Bloomington, IN: Solution Tree Press, 2011), 50–51; Linda Darling-Hammond et al., "Professional Learning in the Learning Profession: A Status Report on Teacher Development in the U.S. and Abroad" (Dallas, TX, National Staff Development Council, 2009), 9; Lawrence Leonard and Pauline Leonard, "The Continuing Trouble with Collaboration: Teachers Talk," *Current Issues in Education* 6, no. 15 (2003), http://cie.asu.edu/volume6/number15/index.html; David J. Flinders, "Teacher Isolation and the New Reform," *Journal of Curriculum and Supervision* 4, no. 1 (1988), 17–29; Dan C. Lortie, *Schoolteacher: A Sociological Study* (Chicago: University of Chicago Press, 1975), 14–16 and 96–98.

5. Darling-Hammond et al., "Professional Learning," 4; Richard DuFour and Robert Eaker, *Professional Learning Communities at Work* (Bloomington, IN: Solution Tree Press, 1998), 16.

6. Fred M. Newmann and Gary G. Wehlage, "Successful School Restructuring: A Report to the Public and Educators by the Center on Organization and Restructuring of Schools" (Madison, WI: Wisconsin Center for Education Research, 1997), 28–40.

7. Darling-Hammond et al., "Professional Learning," 6.

8. Leonard and Leonard, "The Continuing Trouble."

9. Fred M. Newmann et al., "Instructional Program Coherence: What It Is and Why It Should Guide School Improvement Policy," *Education Evaluation and Policy Analysis* 23, no. 4 (2011): 305.

10. Ibid., 301.

11. Ibid., 297–298.

12. Ibid., 311.

Chapter 4

1. Douglas B. Reeves, *Finding Your Leadership Focus: Transforming Professional Learning into Student Results, K–12* (Thousand Oaks, CA: Corwin Press, 2011), 14.
2. Stephen R. Covey, *The 8th Habit: From Effectiveness to Greatness*, (New York: Free Press, 2004), 160.
3. Created by P. David Pearson and Margaret C. Gallagher, the *Gradual Release of Responsibility* is a method in which the responsibility for a task is gradually shifted from teacher to student. See P. David Pearson and Margaret C. Gallagher, "The instruction of reading comprehension," *Contemporary Educational Psychology* 8, no. 3 (1983): 317–344.
4. Douglas B. Reeves, "Pull the Weeds Before You Plant the Flowers," *Educational Leadership* 64, no. 1 (2006): 89–90.
5. Kathryn Parker Boudett, Elizabeth A. City, and Richard J. Murnane, eds., *Data Wise: A Step-by-Step Guide to Using Assessment Results to Improve Teaching and Learning* (Cambridge, MA: Harvard Education Press, 2005).

Chapter 5

1. Meredith I. Honig et al., "Central Office Transformation for District-wide Teaching and Learning Improvement," Center for the Study of Teaching and Policy (Seattle: University of Washington, 2010), 5.
2. Michael Fullan, "The Change Leader," *Educational Leadership* 59, no. 8 (2002), 16–20.
3. Kathryn Parker Boudett, Elizabeth A. City, and Richard J. Murnane, eds., *Data Wise: A Step-by-Step Guide to Using Assessment Results to Improve Teaching and Learning* (Cambridge, MA: Harvard Education Press, 2005).
4. Wendy Togneri and Stephen E. Anderson, "Beyond Islands of Excellence: What Districts Can Do to Improve Instruction and Achievement in All Schools," Learning First Alliance (Washington, DC: Association for Supervision and Curriculum Development, 2003), 6.
5. Ibid., "Beyond Islands," 9.
6. Diane Massell, "The District Role in Building Capacity: Four Strategies," CPRE Policy Briefs (Philadelphia: Consortium for Policy Research in Education, 2000), 3–4.
7. Jerry J. Bellon, Elner C. Bellon, and Mary Ann Blank, *Teaching from a Research Knowledge Base: A Development and Renewal Process* (New York: Macmillan, 1992), 277–278.

Chapter 6

1. Linda Darling-Hammond et al., "Professional Learning in the Learning Profession: A Status Report on Teacher Development in the U.S. and Abroad" (Dallas, TX, National Staff Development Council, 2009), 5–6.
2. Kathryn Parker Boudett, Elizabeth A. City, and Richard J. Murnane, eds., *Data Wise: A Step-by-Step Guide to Using Assessment Results to Improve Teaching and Learning* (Cambridge, MA: Harvard Education Press, 2005).
3. Ed Catmull, "How Pixar Fosters Collective Creativity," *Harvard Business Review* 86, no. 9 (2008): 1–10.

4. Joseph P. McDonald et al., *The Power of Protocols*, (New York: Teachers College Press, 2007), 63–66.

5. Darling-Hammond et al., "Professional Learning," 11; Lawrence Leonard and Pauline Leonard, "The Continuing Trouble with Collaboration: Teachers Talk," *Current Issues in Education* 6, no. 15 (2003), http://cie.asu.edu/volume6/number15/index.html; David J. Flinders, "Teacher Isolation and the New Reform," *Journal of Curriculum and Supervision* 4, no. 1 (1988), 17–29; Dan C. Lortie, *Schoolteacher: A Sociological Study*, (Chicago: University of Chicago Press, 1975), 14–16, 96–98.

Chapter 7

1. Mary M. Kennedy, *Inside Teaching: How Classroom Life Undermines Reform* (Cambridge, MA: Harvard University Press, 2005), 3.

2. Kathryn Parker Boudett, Elizabeth A. City, and Richard J. Murnane, eds., *Data Wise: A Step-by-Step Guide to Using Assessment Results to Improve Teaching and Learning* (Cambridge, MA: Harvard Education Press, 2005).

Chapter 8

1. Kathryn Parker Boudett, Elizabeth A. City, and Richard J. Murnane, eds., *Data Wise: A Step-by-Step Guide to Using Assessment Results to Improve Teaching and Learning* (Cambridge, MA: Harvard Education Press, 2005).

Chapter 9

1. Gina and her colleagues attended the Data Wise Summer Institute at the Harvard Graduate School of Education (HGSE). For more information on HGSE's Programs in Professional Education, visit http://www.gse.harvard.edu/ppe.

2. The CUSD leaders selected consultants from Education Direction to partner with them in leading their schools through the implementation of a data-driven inquiry cycle. To maintain a focus on the practices of the district, we will refer to ourselves as the outside provider in third person throughout this chapter, as we have in previous chapters.

Afterword

1. Mary M. Kennedy, *Inside Teaching: How Classroom Life Undermines Reform* (Cambridge, MA: Harvard University Press, 2005), 3; Martin Carnoy, Richard Elmore, and Leslie Santee Siskin, eds., *The New Accountability: High Schools and High-Stakes Testing* (New York: RoutledgeFalmer, 2003), vi; Larry Cuban and Michael Usdan, eds., *Powerful Reforms with Shallow Roots: Improving America's Urban Schools* (New York: Teachers College Press, 2003), 180; Richard F. Elmore, "Change and Improvement in Educational Reform," in *A Nation Reformed?: American Education 20 Years After A Nation at Risk*, ed. David T. Gordon (Cambridge, MA: Harvard Education Press, 2003), 227; David Tyack, "Reinventing Schooling," in *Learning From the Past: What History Teaches Us About School Reform*, eds. Diane Ravitch and Maris A. Vinovskis (Baltimore: Johns Hopkins University Press, 1995), 193.

2. Tyack, "Reinventing Schooling," 192.

3. Kennedy, *Inside Teaching*, 3.

4. David T. Gordon, introduction to *A Nation Reformed?: American Education 20 Years After A Nation at Risk*, ed. David T. Gordon (Cambridge, MA: Harvard Education Press, 2003), 6.

5. Mike Schmoker, *Results Now: How We Can Achieve Unprecedented Improvements in Teaching and Learning* (Alexandria, VA: Association for Supervision and Curriculum Development, 2006), 109; John E. Chubb and Terry M. Moe, "Better Schools Through New Institutions: Giving Americans Choice," in *The Jossey-Bass Reader on School Reform* (San Francisco: Jossey-Bass, 2001), 524; Diane Ravitch, "Reformers, Radicals, Romantics," in *The Jossey-Bass Reader on School Reform* (San Francisco: Jossey-Bass, 2001), 80; Linda Darling-Hammond, *The Right to Learn: A Blueprint for Creating Schools That Work* (San Francisco: Jossey-Bass, 1997), 19–20.

6. Darling-Hammond, *The Right to Learn*, 66.

7. Chubb and Moe, "Better Schools," 524.

8. Meredith I. Honig and Thomas C. Hatch, "Crafting Coherence: How Schools Strategically Manage Multiple, External Demands," *Educational Researcher* 33 (8): 16.

9. Kathryn Parker Boudett, Elizabeth A. City, and Richard J. Murnane, eds., *Data Wise: A Step-by-Step Guide to Using Assessment Results to Improve Teaching and Learning* (Cambridge, MA: Harvard Education Press, 2005).

10. Amanda Datnow, "Happy Marriage or Uneasy Alliance? The Relationship Between Comprehensive School Reform and State Accountability Systems," *Journal of Education for Students Placed at Risk* 10 (1): 113–138; Fullan, *The New Meaning of Educational Change* (New York: Teachers College Press, 2001), 221.

11. Robert Evans, "The Culture of Resistance," in *The Jossey-Bass Reader on School Reform* (San Francisco: Jossey-Bass, 2001), 524.

12. Vivian Troen and Katherine C. Boles, *Who's Teaching Your Children?* (New Haven, CT: Yale University Press, 2003), 93–140.

13. Linda Darling-Hammond et al., "Professional Learning in the Learning Profession: A Status Report on Teacher Development in the U.S. and Abroad" (Dallas, TX, National Staff Development Council, 2009), 5.

14. Ibid., "Professional Learning." 3.

ACKNOWLEDGMENTS

Without the support and encouragement of our colleagues at Education Direction (www. EdDirection.com), this project would likely still exist only in our minds and on sticky notes hastily placed in our "book" file folder. This book really came to life when our colleagues proactively suggested we carve out dedicated time for writing. For this gift of time, we are indebted to Education Direction.

The foundation of this book is built upon the experiences of those working on the ground level of school improvement, and specifically inquiry-based school improvement. The district administrators, school leaders, and teachers with whom we have worked in the Chandler Unified School District (CUSD), Evansville Vanderburgh School Corporation (EVSC), and Portland Public Schools (PPS) have enhanced our thinking each step of the way. We hope their commitment to improving teaching and learning is apparent in our writing. Additionally, the educators in hundreds of other districts and schools in which we have worked over the past decade have also informed and contributed to our thinking about the work of school improvement.

Gina Vukovich, Susie Avey, Camille Casteel, and Susan Eissinger in the CUSD deserve special thanks for their unwavering commitment to making the most of Collaborative School Improvement within their district, and for allowing us to be a part of their journey from day one. At EVSC, David Dimmett and Emily Smith-McCormick have worked tirelessly to support schools in CSI, and have remained focused on inquiry-based improvement at the school level. Our partners at EVSC have provided special evidence demonstrating that improving school-level practices begins with improvements in district practices. At PPS, Greg Baker, Vicki Phillips, Carole Smith, John Horn, Jeanine Fukuda, Sue Hiscox, Alan Dichter, and Melissa Goff have made CSI a successful endeavor in Portland by consistently embracing the partnership among the district, the schools engaging in CSI, and supporters from the Nike School Innovation Fund. The Nike School Innovation Fund (www. nikeschoolinnovationfund.org) cocreated and generously financed the school improvement efforts in Portland and served as an inspiring example of how public-private partnerships can make a difference. At Nike, Julia Brim-Edwards, Heidi O'Neill, Trip Randall, and Kimberly Bakken have been instrumental to that partnership's strength.

The Data Wise Project at the Harvard Graduate School of Education has provided the context for inquiry-based school improvement in the districts in which we work (and in thousands of schools across the country). We are particularly indebted to Kathy Boudett, who read early drafts of chapters from this book, offered insightful feedback, and contributed the foreword. Liz City and Richard Murnane—as well as Jennifer Steele, David Ronka, and other *Data Wise* (Harvard Education Press) authors, teachers, and researchers—have created an excellent example of a data-driven school improvement process upon which CSI is built.

Our friend and colleague, Anne Jones, has pushed our thinking perhaps more than any other individual. She has taught us in classrooms and in boardrooms; her ideas have contributed in countless ways, for which we offer our deepest gratitude.

For her many hours reviewing our work with a thoughtful lens, we thank Caroline Chauncey at Harvard Education Press. She provided insightful comments from the book's infancy onward, helping us create a model that will better serve districts. Additionally, two independent reviewers offered comments on our early proposal, which helped us clarify our own thinking and ensure that we developed a work that contributed to the dialogue and resources on school improvement. Cami Hewett, an incredibly talented independent editor, has patiently helped us refine our sometimes-sloppy prose.

Anyone who has undertaken an endeavor of this magnitude knows that our greatest thanks go to those with whom we have the strongest partnership: our colleagues and families.

Trent E. Kaufman

This book represents many years of thinking—from the time I spent as a classroom teacher, principal, graduate student, consultant, and policy analyst to my founding of Education Direction. Across those many roles, I have had the enormous privilege of working with some of the best practitioners and brightest minds in education reform. I am forever indebted to these former and current colleagues, professors, and classmates. It would be difficult to name all of them, but a few stick out as particularly important to my personal and professional development.

Dave Marken believed in me and trusted me with the types of responsibilities that I needed to grow in my early professional years. Larry Cuban's own research and writing, and his assistance with mine, has been enormously influential. Richard Elmore engaged me in a series of conversations and dialogues that still run in my head today. David Ronka was as good a thought-partner in my early strategic thinking as I could have imagined. And Brent Maddin's example constantly reminds me that my passion for education reform definitely has room to grow. My coauthors, Emily and Allison, are great teammates and tireless writers on this project. Without them, this book would still be in my head and not on paper.

And a special thanks to Randy Shumway, who provided the spark (and investment) that birthed Education Direction; while his name is not on the cover of this book, his passion for education and assistance in creating the CSI model is written throughout its pages.

Finally, while I am truly blessed to wake up excited about going to work every day, I am even more enthusiastic when family time approaches. My mom and dad gave me the confidence to try—a gift of inestimable value for a dreamer like me. My children—Philip, Henry, Kate, Isaac, and JT—provide me with immeasurable personal joy and opportunity for self-reflection. And my eternal partner, Rosie, who has no peer in terms of confidence, determination, and work ethic, has made many personal sacrifices for this book. May the return on her investment be improved outcomes for our children and yours.

Emily Dolci Grimm

I couldn't have asked for a better team to share in this work. Thanks to Trent and Allison for pushing my thinking (and for sharing many stories and delicious meals along the way). In my early years in this profession, Alice Lesnick helped me develop a critical lens while sharing in my optimism that we can improve education, a gift I have carried with me throughout this project. Thanks to the two teachers in my life who are also my biggest supporters: Mom and Carole. Through their work, they have illustrated what is possible in education.

Endless thanks and enduring love to David, who is the best trailmate and life partner I could ask for. Thank you for your countless hours of listening patiently to the development of the ideas contained in these pages, for your keen ability to keep life in perspective, and for the laughter (even when I didn't know it was exactly what I needed). I cannot wait to see what the next 2,178.3 miles of our journey together bring.

Allison E. Miller

I would be remiss to start by thanking anyone other than God for giving me the strength and patience it took to complete this project and for the wonderful, supportive individuals (both near and far) He surrounded me with to ensure that this book came to fruition.

I want to acknowledge and thank every teacher that I have had along the way who has taught me to care about education—especially Dr. Jo Carol Mitchell-Rogers, who opened my eyes to the possibilities that exist to make an impact on students' lives. You taught your grasshopper well.

The deepest thanks to all of my family and friends for the integral role that each has played in making me the person that I am today. Thanks go to my children, Elsie and Ollie, for inspiring me to be a better person, even when the days are long. And, last, a special thank you to my husband, Chris, for his constant support of this project (which required him to go above and beyond his normal "super dad" role on occasion) and of every other adventure that he has encouraged me to take on—both in the world of education and beyond.

ABOUT THE AUTHORS

Trent E. Kaufman is the founder and president of Education Direction, a school reform research and consultancy firm. Education Direction serves large public school districts and private organizations seeking to improve teaching and learning. Prior to founding Education Direction, Trent served as a teacher, department chair, technology coordinator, athletics coach, dean of students, assistant principal, and principal in Northern California. He also previously served as a research and teaching fellow for the Harvard Graduate School of Education, a summer fellow for Industry Initiatives in Science and Math Education, a national faculty member for High School Futures, and an analyst for Education Resource Strategies.

Trent earned his doctorate from the Harvard Graduate School of Education in education policy, leadership, and instructional practice. His doctoral research included an analysis of the use of the Balanced Scorecard and other performance management systems as tools for school reform. He earned his master's degree in education leadership from the University of California at Berkeley. Trent has served as a teaching fellow for the *Data Wise* weeklong summer institute as well as the yearlong Harvard *Data Wise* course, is a chapter author of *Data Wise in Action* (Harvard Education Press), and has coauthored a chapter on data-driven decision making in the *Handbook of Research on Educational Communications and Technology* (Springer; in press at time of publication). He has presented at dozens of conferences, including ASCD's annual conference, Learning Forward; the California League of Schools; the Virginia Council for the Social Studies; Brown University's School Leadership Institute; Advanced Academics' Online Learning Leadership Summit; and the California Charter School Association. Trent is a proud parent of five children, the "Cubmaster" in his boys' Cub Scout pack, and an advisor to the Nike School Innovation Fund.

Emily Dolci Grimm has worked as a teacher in both traditional and alternative settings for a decade. She currently works as the Director of School Transformation at Education Direction. Prior to holding this position, Emily served as a teacher, coach, and Response to Intervention (RTI) team member at a high school in Maine. While there, she secured grant funding to create and implement the Girls' Aspirations Program, an alternative education program to meet the needs of at-risk girls in the community.

Emily earned her bachelor's degree from Haverford College and is currently working toward her master's degree in school leadership from the University of Utah. She is a certified CASA volunteer (guardian *ad litem*) and an avid hiker and skier. She recently completed a five-month thru-hike of the Appalachian Trail from Maine to Georgia and looks forward to someday hiking the Pacific Crest Trail with her husband.

Allison E. Miller currently serves as the Director of Professional Development at Education Direction. With over a decade of classroom teaching experience, she is passionate about education and literacy. Prior to working with Education Direction, Allison served in a variety of capacities at public and private schools in South Carolina and Georgia. She has worked as a classroom teacher and program director, as well as a private educational consultant for students with learning disabilities. In addition, Allison has written and implemented curricula for two visual arts programs. She is certified in art education, holds a license as a reading specialist, and is trained in both the Orton-Gillingham and Wilson teaching approaches.

Allison earned her master's degree in education from the Harvard Graduate School of Education, where her focus of study was language and literacy, and a bachelor of arts in art education from Anderson University. She currently serves as an advisor to the Deseret News Reading Literacy Board. In addition, she is an active member of the Learning Disabilities Association and the International Reading Association. Allison enjoys hiking and biking in Park City, Utah, with her husband and two children.

INDEX